MOSQUITO PHOTO-RECONNAISSANCE UNITS OF WORLD WAR 2

SERIES EDITOR: TONY HOLMES

OSPREY COMBAT AIRCRAFT • 13

MOSQUTTO PHOTO-RECONNAISSANCE UNITS OF WORLD WAR 2

Martin Bowman

OSPREY
AVIATION

Front cover

PR XVI NS851/H of No 680 Sqn is depicted here undertaking a PR sortie from Foggia, in Italy, in 1944. This particular unit was initially equipped with Spitfires for PR duties, but on 17 February 1944 it received the first (MM297) of nine PR XVIs at its Matariya base, outside Cairo. The Mosquitoes were duly allocated to the 1st Detachment at Tocra, under the command of Wg Cdr J R Whelan. On 7 May No 680 Sqn flew its first Mosquito PR sortie when MM333 (piloted by Flt Lt A M Yelland) covered ports and airfields as far away as Salonika and Larissa, in Greece. Throughout 1944, B Flight mostly covered Greece and the Balkans, as well as central and southern Europe – when fitted with 100-gal drop tanks, the PR XVI boasted a range of over 2000 miles. In August 1944 a detachment from the squadron moved to San Severo in order to fly PR sorties to Austria, Bavaria and Yugoslavia. By the end of the year, PR XVIs equipped both A and B Flights, which covered southern Germany, Austria and Czechoslovakia, as well as the eastern Mediterranean. Following the loss of several Mosquitoes to enemy fighters (as well as so-called 'friendly' fighters) in early 1944, a P-51 escort was provided by the Fifteenth Air Force's 31st Fighter Group. In order to make the Mosquitoes more easily recognisable for Allied fighter pilots, No 680 Sqn applied red and white tail stripes to their PR XVIs from the spring of 1944 onwards
(*cover artwork by Iain Wyllie*)

For a catalogue of all titles published by Osprey Military, Aviation or Automotive please write to:
The Marketing Manager, Osprey Publishing Limited, P.O. Box 140, Wellingborough, Northants NN8 4ZA, United Kingdom

Or visit our website:
www.ospreypublishing.com

First published in Great Britain in 1999 by Osprey Publishing
Elms Court, Chapel Way, Botley, Oxford, OX2 9LP

ISBN 1 85532 891 7

Edited by Tony Holmes
Page design by TT Designs, T & B Truscott
Cover Artwork by Iain Wyllie
Aircraft Profiles by Chris Davey
Figure Artwork by Mike Chappell
Scale Drawings by Mark Styling

Origination by Valhaven Ltd, Isleworth, UK
Printed through Bookbuilders, Hong Kong

00 01 02 03   10 9 8 7 6 5 4 3 2

EDITOR'S NOTE

To make this best-selling series as authoritative as possible, the editor would be extremely interested in hearing from any individual who may have relevant photographs, documentation or first-hand experiences relating to the elite pilots, and their aircraft, of the various theatres of war. Any material used will be fully credited to its original source. Please write to Tony Holmes at 10 Prospect Road, Sevenoaks, Kent, TN13 3UA, Great Britain.

ACKNOWLEDGEMENTS

The author wishes to thank the following individuals for their valued assistance during the compilation of this volume: Steve Adams; Peter R Arnold; Eric Atkins DFC* KW*, RAF Retd, Chairman, Mosquito Aircrew Association; Air Marshal Sir A H W 'Freddie' Ball KCB CB DSO DFC; Frank Baylis AFM CdG* KC; Mike Bailey; Andy Bird; Philip Birtles; Terence Boughton; Denis Coram; Wg Cdr David Cox, RAF Retd; Allan L Davies; George J French; Ken Godfrey; Eric Hill DFC DFM; Gordon E Hughes, RAF Retd; Lawrence K 'Kev' Kevan DFC; Philip Jarrett; Arthur T Kirk-Waring DFC; Edward Leaf; Ron MacKay; Bill McClintock; the late Denis Moore; Win Moore; John R Myles DFC AM RCAF; Wg Cdr Ken H Pickup, RAF Retd; H C S 'Sandy' Powell DFC; Beth Prescott; Gordon Puttick DFC; C R Mickey Randles, RAF Retd; Jerry Scutts; George Sesler; Graham M Simons; Ray Smith DFM; Gerald Stevens DFC; Andy Thomas; Geoff Thomas; Joe Townshend DFM; Sqn Ldr Cyril Turner, RAF Retd; Paddy Walker, USAF Retd; George Watson DFC; Jill Wharton; Gordon White; W J 'Bill' White RCAF DFC; John J Winship DFC, RCAF Retd; and Gerry R Wooll, RCAF.

CONTENTS

BLUE BIRDS OVER THE WHITE CLIFFS

'The military organisation with the most efficient photographic reconnaissance will win the next war', said Gen von Fritsch, later Chief of the German General Staff, in 1938. The first British PR sortie over Germany, flown on 10 March 1939, was performed by one of two converted Lockheed Model 12As bought for the purpose, and stationed at Heston. The pilot, Australian Sidney Cotton, and his co-pilot, photographed Mannheim. In an effort to disguise its true intent, Cotton's unit was named the Special Survey Flight. On Saturday, 2 September 1939 – the day before Britain declared war on Germany – the Lockheed 12A of the Heston Flight, as it was now known, sortied over the River Elbe. In November 1939 the Heston Flight became No 2 Camouflage Unit, and in mid-January 1940 was again renamed the Photographic Development Unit, or simply the PDU. Finally, in July 1940, it became the PRU (Photographic Reconnaissance Unit).

What the PRU badly needed was an aircraft not only capable of carrying multi-camera installations, but which was faster than the Blenheim and able to photograph areas beyond the range of a PR Spitfire. Ever since 1938, the de Havilland company at Hatfield had been trying, without success, to convince the Air Ministry that its unarmed, DH 98 (Mosquito) bomber, which was to be mostly built of wood, and had a crew of only two, could operate successfully in hostile skies without the need for defensive armament. The company argued that the DH 98's superior speed was its best defensive weapon against enemy fighters. Late

W4051 was the last of three Mosquito prototypes to fly, on 10 June 1941. The fuselage originally intended for this aircraft was used to replace W4050's fuselage, which had been fractured in a tail wheel incident, and so W4051 received a production fuselage instead – a factor which enabled this prototype to fly operational sorties with the PRU (*via Philip Jarrett*)

in 1939 there was still strong opposition to any unarmed bomber version, but the AOC-in-C, Bomber Command, conceded that there was a need for a fast, unarmed, reconnaissance aircraft, equipped with three F24 cameras. It was agreed that a two-man crew in any reconnaissance version put forward by de Havilland was acceptable (although at first the Air Ministry wanted them seated in tandem).

On 1 March 1940 a contract was placed with de Havilland for 50 DH 98 aircraft, including 19 PR versions. Work began on the Mosquito prototypes, the first (E-0234, later W4050) flying on 25 November 1940. By January 1941 W4050 was proving faster than a Spitfire in tests at 6000 ft, and by February it was recording speeds of around 390 mph at 22,000 ft. PR prototype W4051 was the second Mosquito completed at Salisbury Hall. While it retained the short engine nacelles and tailplane of the prototype, it differed in having longer wings (by 20 in), and carried three vertical cameras and one oblique. At first the camera mounts were made of steel, but these were later changed to wood, as these helped reduce camera vibration and improve image quality.

The nightfighter prototype became the second Mosquito to fly when the fuselage originally intended for W4051 was used to replace W4050's fuselage, which had fractured at Boscombe Down in a tail wheel incident. W4051 received a production fuselage instead, which later enabled the prototype to fly on operations – it completed its maiden flight on 10 June 1941. Eleven days later, the Air Ministry decided that nine aircraft (W4064-72) from the 19 originally ordered on 1 March 1940 as PR versions should be converted to unarmed bombers, and these came to be known as the PRU/Bomber Conversion Type, or B IV Series I.

On 13 July 1941 W4051 was flown to Oxfordshire by Geoffrey de Havilland and handed over to No 1 PRU at Benson, which was then commanded by Wg Cdr G W Tuttle OBE, DFC, where it became the first Mosquito to be taken on charge by the RAF. W4054 and W4055 followed on 22 July and 8 August respectively. Beginning in September, No 1 PRU received seven more production PR Is – W4056 and W4058-63 (W4057 became the B V bomber prototype). Four of these (W4060-63) were later modified with increased fuel tankage for long range operations and two, (W4062 and W4063) were tropicalised.

On 13 July 1941 W4051 was handed over to No 1 PRU at Benson, where it became the first Mosquito to be taken on charge by the RAF. It was one of four PR Is transferred to operate from Wick, in Scotland, and on 20 February 1942 it was flown to the Franco-Spanish border, and marshalling yards and airfields at Toulouse, in southern France (*via Philip Jarrett*)

Long range fuel tanks installed in the bomb-bay of four PR Is (W4060-W4063) enabled them to fly long range operations over Europe (*via GMS*)

The standard Mosquito camera installation at the time consisted of three vertical cameras, namely the F24 Universal oblique camera for day and night photography, the F52 20- or 36-in high altitude day reconnaissance camera (which entered service in May 1942) and the American K17 survey and mapping camera with 6-in lens, plus a single F24 camera mounted in the lower fuselage. The fit depended on the type of mission flown, with one of the most widely used being a single K17 (or K8AB with 12-in lens) forward and a split vertical F52 installation behind the wing, and an F24 oblique camera facing to port.

This was sometimes changed to a split vertical F52 camera installation forward, two standard vertical F52 cameras and one F24 aft of the wing. The split vertical camera installation was basically two cameras (F24s or F52s) mounted at slightly differing angles to double the field of view, while retaining the 60 per cent overlap needed for stereoscopic coverage of the target area. The split vertical F52 36-in camera installation gave the PR I lateral coverage of three miles from 35,000 ft and 255 mph. Besides these installations, some late model PR Mosquitoes were fitted with two forward-facing F24 14-in lens cameras – one in each dummy 50-gal drop tank – for low-level photography.

Each of the early PR Is was named after a different variety of strong liquor, W4055 being christened Benedictine and others Whiskey and Vodka, Drambuie, Cointreau and Creme de Menthe.

During tests on 16 September 1941, W4055's generator packed up over the Bay of Biscay, and with no power to drive the cameras, 25-year old Sqn Ldr Rupert Clerke (an old Etonian) and 32-year old Sgt Sowerbutts (a pre-war Margate barber) were forced to abandon the sortie. They were pursued by three Bf 109s, but the PR I easily outpaced them at 23,000 ft and returned safely.

Sqn Ldr Clerke and Sgt Sowerbutts made the first successful Mosquito PR I sortie the next day when they set out in W4055 at 1130 hrs for a daylight photo reconnaissance of Brest, La Pallice and Bordeaux, before arriving back at Benson at 1745 hours. On the 20th Flt Lt Alastair L 'Ice' Taylor DFC and his navigator, Sgt Sidney E Horsfall, successfully photographed Bordeaux, Pauillac, Le Verdon and La Pallice. Taylor was a brilliant PR Spitfire and Mosquito pilot, who specialised in 'dicing' (low level PR of specific targets). The third flight was made when Taylor

Sqn Ldr Alastair L 'Ice' Taylor DFC, and two bars, was a brilliant PR Spitfire and Mosquito pilot who specialised in 'dicing' (low-level PR of specific targets). On 4 December 1941, Taylor, who by now had become the first PR pilot to fly over 100 sorties, was lost, along with his navigator, Sgt Sidney E Horsfall, in W4055 on a sortie to Trondheim and Bergen

W4059 flew 59 PR sorties in No 1 PRU before joining No 540 Sqn in October 1942. On 2 March 1942 W4059 photographed the *Gneisenau*, and on 24 April Flg Off Victor Ricketts and Sgt Boris Lukhmanoff used W4059 to take photos of the Lancaster daylight raid on the MAN works at Augsburg

In 1942 St Nazaire possessed the only dry dock outside Germany large enough to take a vessel the size of the *Tirpitz*, so on 27 March Operation *Chariot* was undertaken to knock it out. Following a six-mile voyage up the Loire, HMS *Campbeltown* was successfully rammed and lodged into the entrance lock to the Bassin de Penhouet. Twenty-four hours later, the charges inside the ship exploded and completely dislodged the outer lock gate, rendering the dry dock useless. PR photos taken by Flt Lt John Merrifield in W4051, and others from W4060, were used to brief and train the Combined Operations force hours before the raiding party left England. They showed four *Miwe*-class MTBs berthed alongside the exact spot Lt Col A C Newman had chosen as his command post, which allowed him to alter his plans accordingly. This photograph, in March 1943, shows the U-boat pens (top), and the wreck of the scuttled *Campbeltown* inside the dry dock (*IWM*)

and Horsfall covered Heligoland and Sylt in W4055 *Benedictine*.

After proving their worth over northern France, W4051, W4055, W4059 and W4061 were transferred to operate from Wick, in Scotland, with Sqn Ldr Taylor in command. In October 1941 the PR I Mosquitoes carried out 16 successful sorties to Norway.

On 4 December, Taylor, who by now was the first PR pilot to fly over 100 sorties, with Horsfall, flew W4055 on a PR sortie to cover Trondheim and Bergen, but they failed to return. It is thought that after they were badly shot up by new German high level anti-aircraft guns, Taylor put down in the sea to prevent the aircraft falling into enemy hands. After 88 sorties, this was the first loss of a PR Mosquito. By December the unit had moved to Leuchars, near the Firth of Forth. The new base proved more suited to PR operations, greatly reducing the time taken to send photos to the Central Interpretation Unit at RAF Medmenham.

Unkindly referred to by pilots outside the unit as 'Pilots Rest Unit', No 1 PRU was anything but, and its operational cycle was about to become even more far reaching. On 15 January 1942, Flt Lt John R H Merrifield overflew Gydnia, in Poland, and Danzig, in eastern Germany, in W4061, but his targets were obscured by cloud. Two days earlier a PR I was sent out to Malta for trials in the Mediterranean. However, the aircraft, piloted by Flg Off Kelly, was written off in a crash-landing on arrival at Luqa. A second Mosquito, piloted by Plt Off Walker, arrived safely on Malta on 17 January, and after a series of sorties over Italy, it was lost on

The aircraft carrier *Graf Zeppelin* alongside the west bank of the River Oder, at Stettin. On 2 June 1942 Plt Offs Robin Sinclair and Nelson used PR I W4060, fitted with the new 36-in F 52 camera, to obtain photos of the *Graf Zeppelin* and the battleship *Scharnhorst* in port at Gydnia (*IWM*)

PR I W4060, which Flg Off Victor Ricketts and Sgt Boris Lukhmanoff used on 2 March 1942 to photograph the *Scharnhorst* undergoing repairs at Wilhelmshaven. W4060 also photographed the French coast prior to the commando raid on St Nazaire, and was used by Ricketts and Lukhmanoff to photograph the Renault factory at Boulogne-Billancourt immediately after the raid by 235 bombers on the night of 3/4 March. On 7 July Flg Off K H Bayley and Plt Off Little of H Flight at Leuchars took off in W4060 at 1230 for Wick to top up their tanks before heading for Norway to photograph the *Tirpitz*, but they were forced to return to base when the long-range immersed fuel pump failed to function. The starboard undercarriage leg collapsed on touching down at Leuchars, and the crew tried later to complete the sortie in PR IV DK284. W4060 was lost, along with with David O'Neill and David Lockyer, on 20 February 1943 when it was badly hit by flak and crashed at Loddefjord

31 March after a mission to Sicily. Badly shot up by Bf 109s, Plt Off Kelly and Sgt Pike nursed the ailing Mosquito to Hal Far, where it crashed and burnt out. Both crew survived.

On 20 February 1942 W4051 was flown to the Franco-Spanish border, and over marshalling yards and airfields at Toulouse, in southern France. On 22 February Flt Lt Victor Ricketts and his navigator, Russian

born Sgt Boris Lukhmanoff, covered Cuxhaven and Kiel to take photos of the *Gneisenau* in dry dock there, and on 2 March the same crew (in W4060) photographed the *Scharnhorst* undergoing repairs at Wilhelmshaven, whilst W4059 photographed the *Gneisenau* again. W4060 and W4051 also photographed the French coast prior to the commando raid on St Nazaire, and on 3 March Flt Lt John R H Merrifield successfully returned to the Danzig-Gydnia region.

Although the PRU's first priority remained that of keeping a watch on the *Kriegsmarine*, 1942 would see it being called upon to cover an increasing number of RAF Bomber Command targets. On 14 February 1942 the famous 'area bombing' directive was issued to Bomber Command, and eight days later it became the responsibility of ACM Sir Arthur Harris – the new chief of Bomber Command – to carry it out. Harris immediately questioned the Admiralty's monopoly of PRU operations, and felt that Bomber Command's need was now much greater. On the night of 3/4 March Bomber Command mounted its first

Gydnia pictured on 1 August 1942, showing the battlecruiser *Gneisenau* undergoing repairs, her gun turrets removed, and a large part of her bows cut away

11

TOULON
8 - xi - 42

large-scale raid of the war when it sent 235 bombers to bomb the Renault factory at Boulogne-Billancourt, just west of the centre of Paris. An equally spectacular PR sortie was flown by Ricketts and Luhkmanoff to verify the results.

Flying W4060, they took off from Benson at 1115 hours in heavy rain and thick cloud. and when visibility got worse, Ricketts had to drop down to 900 ft. With Lukhmanoff lying in the nose of the PR I, guiding him, Ricketts resorted to following the twisting River Seine all the way to the capital. They arrived over the burning target at 1230 hours. Lukhmanoff exclaimed, 'Oh Boy! Oh Boy! Did they give the place the works!' There was no time for him to start the cameras as they roared over the wrecked plant, so they banked round and flew across the target for a second time just before it vanished in the mist. They then approached it from another direction, Lukhmanoff making sure they kept away from the 1000-ft high Eiffel Tower! Flying back up the Seine, they had to descend to 400 ft before vainly trying to find the works for the fourth time.

They had been in the target area for 34 minutes now at 400-600 ft, and flak was starting to open up, so Ricketts sped off, climbing to 5000 ft before skimming the waves at zero feet across the Channel still in very poor visibility. After six attempts Ricketts landed at an aerodrome on the south coast at 1415 hours with low-level obliques that are 'dicing' classics. Evidence showed that 300 bombs had fallen on the factory, destroying 31 of 35 buildings. Both Ricketts and Lukhmanoff were decorated for their heroism. In the weeks to come the two men made long-range sorties to Bavaria, Mulhouse and Stuttgart, and used W4059 to take photos of the Lancaster daylight raid on the MAN works at Augsburg on 24 April.

Harris's night bombing offensive was gaining in intensity, and the PRU, as a consequence, had to fly an ever-increasing number of target acquisition and bomb damage assessment sorties. With attrition losses mounting (on 3 April 1942 W4056 was shot down over Stavanger and the crew taken prisoner), more long-range PR aircraft had to be found.

Toulon on 8 November 1942, the day after the *Torch* invasion of North Africa. The port was photographed 11 times by No 540 Sqn between 7-26 November. In port are about 60 ships, including the Vichy French flagship *Strasbourg*, battleship *Provence*, seaplane carrier *Commandant Teste*, battlecruiser *Dunkerque*, cruisers, *Foch* and La *Galissonnïare* and 18 submarines. When the Germans attempted to seize the French Fleet on 27 November it was scuttled on the orders of Admiral de Laborde. Plt Off Hardman and Sgt Cruikshank from Benson subsequently brought back photos showing the sunken ships. With the delivery of two PR Mosquitoes to No 4 PRU in April 1943, sorties were regularly flown, usually from Maison Blanche, to ensure that no attempts were being made to repair any of the crippled vessels (*IWM*)

Accordingly, between April and June 1942, four NF IIs (DD615, 620, 659 and W4089) and two B IV bomber variants (DK284 and 311) were diverted to the PRU as PR IIs and PR IVs, respectively. While the NF IIs lacked long-range tanks, the B IVs boasted bomb-bay tanks and two 50-gall underwing slipper type drop tanks, to give the aircraft a range of 2350 miles – enough to reach northern Norway and back. With three vertical and one oblique cameras installed, Flt Lt Ricketts DFC and Sgt Lukhmanoff performed the first operational sortie in a PR IV on 29 April, using DK284 to over-fly Augsburg, Stuttgart and Saarbrücken in a five-and-a-half-hour flight.

In December 1942 two PR IVs (DZ411 and DZ419 – the latter crashed into the sea off Arbroath, Angus, on 11 July 1943) joined No 540 Sqn, followed, during the first three months of 1943 by a further 27 PR IVs, including DZ383, pictured here in May 1943 – all these aircraft were conversions of existing B IV Series II bombers. DZ383 was finally scrapped on 31 October 1946 (*via Philip Jarrett*)

On 7 May 1942 Ricketts and Lukhmanoff flew the deepest penetration over enemy territory thus far when they used DK284 to photograph Dresden, Pilsen and Regensburg, returning after six hours. On 14 May the unit's CO, Wg Cdr Spencer Ring RCAF made the first operational flight in a PR II when he used DD615 to photograph Alderney. On 25 May, Ricketts and Lukhmanoff overflew Billancourt, Poissy and Le Bourget in this aircraft, and on the 27th, Flt Lt Gerry R Wooll RCAF and Sgt John Fielden also DD615 when they photographed Amiens.

On 24 August, during a sortie to Venice in DK310, Wooll and Fielden suffered an engine failure that resulted in them being interned in Switzerland. On 10 June Ricketts and Lukhmanoff flew a 7^{3}/4-hour sortie to Spezia, Lyons and Marseilles, but their luck finally ran out on 11 July when they were lost in W4089 overflying Strasbourg and Ingolstadt.

Meanwhile, up at Leuchars, May and June 1942 had seen PRU Mosquitoes flying sortie after sortie in an attempt to find and photograph the German battleships berthed in the Norwegian fjords. On 15 May the first PR sortie to the Narvik area was flown by Flg Off Higson in one of the PR IVs, whilst the next day, Flt Lt John Merrifield photographed the *Prinz Eugen* heading south-west, apparently making for Kiel for repairs to damage inflicted by the submarine HMS *Trident*. Forty-eight hours later, Flg Off K H Bayley and Flt Sgt Little took photographs of the *Prinz Eugen* and four destroyers still en route for Kiel. Coverage of Trondheim on 22 and 23 May revealed that the *Tirpitz*, *Admiral Hipper* and *Lützow* were all still berthed in fjords. On 2 June Plt Off Robin Sinclair and Plt Off Nelson (in W4060) used the new 36-in F52 camera to photograph of the aircraft carrier *Graf Zeppelin* and the battleship *Scharnhorst* in Gydnia.

On 7 July 1942 the newly-promoted Flt Lt Bayley and Plt Off Little took off from Leuchars (again in W4060) at 1230 hrs for Wick to top up their tanks before heading for Norway to photograph the *Tirpitz*. However, they were forced to return to base when the long-range immersed fuel pump failed to function. The starboard undercarriage leg collapsed on touch down at Leuchars, and the crew tried later to complete the sortie in PR IV DK284. However, this developed an engine fault and excessively overheated, again forcing the crew to return. They took off for the third time on 7 July, and although an oxygen pipe broke 15 minutes

Flt Lt Bill White, RCAF, and Flt Lt Ron Prescott of No 540 Sqn, who flew their first sortie on 2 December 1942. During December- February 1943, they flew PR sorties over Norway in search of the elusive *Scharnhorst* (Beth Prescott)

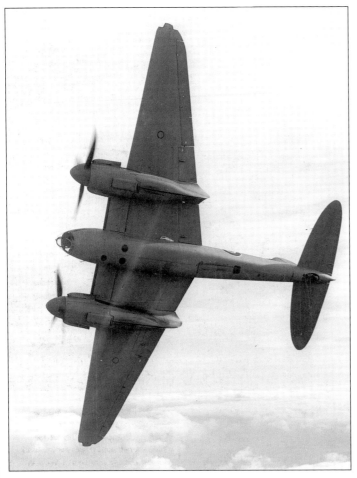

A PR IV reveals its underbelly camera ports as it peels away to starboard (*via Philip Jarrett*)

short of Narvik, they still managed to take an oblique photograph of a destroyer at Bogen and verticals of Bardufoss aerodrome, before the 36-in camera failed at Tromso!

They then sighted the German battle fleet at Arno, in Langfjord, and photographed the battleships, *Tirpitz*, *Scheer* and *Hipper*, seven destroyers, two torpedo boats, three E- or R-boats, and one Altmark tanker from 14,000 ft. They landed at Vaenga, in Russia (a PR detachment was maintained in Russia from mid-August to mid-October 1942), in order to refuel, and after lunch on the 8th, took off for home. Bayley and Little finally landed at 2050 with their valuable photos.

On 19 October 1942 No 1 PRU was reformed at Benson as five PR squadrons. Three of them were equipped with Spitfires, while H and L Flights at Leuchars were merged to form No 540 (Mosquito) Sqn, under the command of Sqn Ldr M J B Young DFC. No 544 Sqn (which was equipped mostly with Wellingtons and Spitfires, but eventually replaced these in March 1943 with PR IV and PR IX Mosquitoes) was formed under the command of Sqn Ldr W R Alcott DFC. In December 1942 two PR IVs (DZ411 and 419) joined No 540 Sqn, followed, during the first three months of 1943, by a further 27 PR IVs – all conversions of existing B IVs. PRU training unit, No 8(PR) OTU, was also established at Fraserburgh, Aberdeenshire, with Wg Cdr Lord Malcolm Douglas-Hamilton as its CO.

Various No 540 Sqn detachments were made to Malta (on 1 October 1942, Plt Off McKay made the first return trip to the island, returning to Benson on the 4th) and Gibraltar. However, in the main, No 540 photographed German capital ships in Baltic waters and in North German ports, and carried out BDA and target reconnaissance.

Serviceability of aircraft in the winter of 1942-43 was only 50 per cent at times because of water seepage into badly fitted No 7 bulkheads. Late in 1942 the first of five PR VIIIs (which began as B IV Series II aircraft, with 1,565hp two-stage- supercharged Merlin 61 engines in place of the 21/22) began to reach No 540 Sqn, this version being built to fill the gap until deliveries of the PR IX and PR XVI were made.

The PR VIII had a greatly improved ceiling, which allowed PR Mosquitoes to operate at high altitude for the first time. DK324, which first flew on 20 October 1942, was a prototype for the Mk VIII version, and it reached No 540 for testing on 28 November 1942. DZ342 arrived on 15 December 1942, followed in 1943 by DZ364 on 22 January, DZ404 on 4 February and DZ424 on 28 March.

The first PR VIII sortie was flown on 19 February 1943 when Sqn Ldr Gordon E Hughes and Sgt H W Evans (in DZ342) overflew La Rochelle and St Nazaire, although they were unable to take any photos because the mud flap over the camera lens failed to open. The first successful PR VIII sorties therefore took place on 27 February when Flt Lt K H Bayley DFC flew DZ364 to Frankfurt on a bomb damage assessment flight, and DZ342 covered Emden and Bremen. On 8 March unit CO, Wg Cdr M J B Young (in DZ364), became the first Mosquito pilot to photograph Berlin (this aircraft was subsequently lost, along with Flt Sgt M Custance and his navigator, on 18 March 1943).

A heavy bomber raid on the V2 preparation and launch site at Watten, France, on 7 September 1943 devastated the complex, and forced the Germans to concentrate development at Wizernes. This site was also attacked and destroyed by Lancasters of No 617 Sqn on 17 July 1944. This low-level oblique taken after the attack shows the great concrete dome, and the access tunnel, which has been narrowly missed

On 2 December 1942, 22-year old Canadian pilot Flt Lt Bill White, and his navigator, 23-year old Flt Lt Ron Prescott, flew their first operation (a short trip lasting 2 hr 30 min to Bergen in DK311) since joining No 540 Sqn. Prior to this, they had had a close call during a training flight in DD615 on 18 November when, at about 15,000 ft, the starboard engine blew off a flame trap. When smoke began pouring from the rear of the engine White shut it down, feathered the prop, and activated the fire extinguisher. This had little effect, and by the time they were down to a few thousand feet over Mount Farm, flames were visibly issuing from the rear of the wing. Concerned that the fuel tanks might blow, and by this time over the airfield, they decided to land rather than bale out. They crash landed at Mount Farm, where the right undercarriage leg fell off, but both men walked away virtually unscathed.

During December, White and Prescott flew two five-hour operations over Norway in W4060 (which was the first long-range version of the PR I), and on 12 January 1943 they flew a 3hr 55 min flight in the same aircraft in an attempt to locate the harbour where the *Scharnhorst* was at anchor. However, despite flying over an area of coast between Statlandet to Lister, nothing was seen. On 24 January, again in W4060, they searched between Grimstadt Fjord-Bergen-Odda and Stavanger, where they were fired on by German flak, but again nothing was found. On the 26th, in W4059, they searched from Sogne Fjord down to Stavanger, flying at 3000 ft, again without result! Two more flights were made in February, on the 2nd and the 5th, and on these sorties the search area was extended north from Statlandet to Trondheim. Each flight lasted for over five hours, and on the 5th they flew in 10/10ths cloud almost all the way.

Koningsburg, as photographed by Flt Lt Morgan and Sgt Baylis on their 36th sortie on 15 September 1944 in PR XVI MM303. Baylis recalls; 'The sortie was unusual because we flew to RAF Coltishall first, to refuel there and obtain optimum fuel for range, as we intended to carry on to the Italian airfield of San Severo, on the plain near Foggia. It was a long haul to East Prussia, but the target was clear, and all briefed photography was accomplished. We left the area on a southerly heading, passing east of Lodz and observing the Americans supplying Warsaw in the distance. We landed at San Severo just as the dusk was deepening' (*Baylis Collection*)

On 16 February the weather was not predicted accurately, and their flight in DK311, again to Norway, proved to be extremely hazardous and required great skill, as Bill White remembers;

'Since we preferred to stay just under the altitude at which we produced contrails, we did most of our flights between 20,000 and 30,000 ft. in the belly of the aircraft we had two 36-in cameras, which took line overlap pictures. These produced 3-D views of the areas being photographed, which were then examined by our intelligence people. Details as small as a golf ball were detectable. We also carried a smaller camera in the port side of the aircraft, and with this we could take oblique pictures. Some of the trips involved low-level photography. and this required flying at tree-top level. On 15 May we were jumped by six Bf 109s while flying photo runs over Oslo. The '109 was faster than us in a climb or a dive, but the Mosquito could out-turn them.

'With the excellent direction by Ron, we were able to do ever decreasing turns and avoid their gunfire. We were also able to inch our way over to Sweden. The Swedes will never know how grateful we were to them as they opened up with every flak battery on their coast. The Ack-Ack was always behind us, and I'll never know how many '109s they got. The return to Leuchars was just a normal flight from Sweden, with no problems from fighters.'

On their 22nd sortie, flown on 22 April 1943 in DZ473, Bill White and Ron Prescott completed one of the most memorable flights of their extensive operational careers. They were sent to photograph the railyards at Stettin, which is Germany's biggest Baltic port, and which had been bombed two days before on the night of the full moon – 20/21 April – by 339 'heavies', as well as the Politz oil refinery and Swinemünde, on the Baltic coast. Twenty-four fires were still burning at Stettin when the PR aircraft flew over the target a day-and-a-half later, approximately 100 acres in the centre of the town having been devastated. Bill White recalls;

'On leaving Stettin, we left our cameras running all down the north coast of Germany, and when the film was developed, it was found to contain pictures of Peenemünde.'

The interpreters of the CIU (Central Intelligence Unit) at Medmenham studied the photos brought back by the crew. From the type of buildings seen, and the elliptical earthworks (originally photographed in May 1942) that were also present, they concluded that Peenemünde must be an experimental centre, probably connected with explosives and propellants. One of the prints from the 22 April 1943 sortie showed an object 25 ft long projecting from what was thought to be a service building, although it had mysteriously disappeared on the next frame!

A sortie flown on 14 May 1943 by Sqn Ldr Gordon Hughes and Flt Sgt John R Chubb brought back more photos, and further investigation of the photos from the 22 April sortie revealed that road vehicles and railway wagons near one of the earthworks were carrying cylindrical objects measuring about 38 ft long. On 17 May it was concluded

In September 1944 Flt Lt Morgan and Sgt Baylis performed two low-level flights around Normandy and western France just to obtain photos of the destruction left behind after the Allies had passed. The first, on 25 September, covered St Quentin, Cambrai, Douai, Lens, St Omer, Boulogne, Watten and Wizernes. The shadow of Morgan and Baylis's PR XVI MM307 can be seen as it passes over a devastated factory (*Frank Baylis Collection*)

that German rocket development had not only probably been underway for some time, but was also 'far advanced'.

A sixth sortie to Peenemünde on 2 June 1943 in DZ419 unearthed scant new information, but ten days later a sortie flown by Flt Lt Reggie A Lenton (in DZ473) resulted in the first definite evidence that the previously unidentified objects were in fact V2 rockets – one was photographed near to a building adjacent to one of the elliptical earthworks lying horizontally on a trailer. On 23 June Flt Sgt E P H Peek brought back photos so clear that two rockets could be seen lying on road vehicles inside the elliptical earthwork. The news was relayed immediately to Prime Minister Winston Churchill. PRU Mosquitoes photographed Peenemünde again on 27 June, and 22 and 26 July.

It was now almost certain that Hitler was preparing a rocket offensive against southern England, and it had to be forestalled with all speed. On 17/18 August 1943 596 Lancasters, Halifaxes and Stirlings set out to destroy the experimental rocket site. Forty aircraft were lost, but 560 bombers reduced the target to rubble by dropping almost 1800 tons of bombs. Next morning Flg Off R A Hosking of No 540 Sqn (in LR413) reconnoitered the target area, and returned again the following day. The raid had put the production of V2 rockets back by at least two months.

Although the attack forced the Germans to relocate development and production of V2s to an underground facility in Austria, raids continued against secret weapons' sites in France, including the V2 preparation and launch site at Watten, which was bombed by the USAAF on 27 August. A PRU sortie three days later revealed that the target was not completely destroyed, so a follow-up raid was flown on 7 September, which devastated the complex and forced the Germans to concentrate development at Wizernes (this site was in turn attacked and destroyed by Lancasters of No 617 Sqn on 17 July 1944). While PR never did reveal how the V2s were launched (ground intelligence showed that they were to be launched vertically), during October 1944–March 1945, No 544 Sqn Mosquitoes, and other PR aircraft, identified several launching sites in Holland.

PR was much more successful in identifying the existence and launching sites of Germany's other secret weapons, however. It all began by chance on 28 November 1943 when a Mosquito from Leuchars, flown by Sqn Ldr John Merrifield DSO DFC and his navigator, Flg Off W N Whalley, set out to photo-graph bomb damage in Berlin. They reached the German capital, but were unable to take any photographs

because of the low cloud cover. Merrifield then turned north, back towards the Baltic coast, to cover secondary targets that he had been given at briefing. There were shipping targets at Stettin and Swinemünde, airfields and a suspected radar installation at Zinnovitz (Zempin) on an island which is separated from the mainland by the River Peene. Merrifield covered each location in turn, and realising that he still had film left, overflew Peenemünde airfield, before returning home.

When the film was developed, the shots of Zinnovitz showed buildings that were similar in size and shape to those which had been photographed at Bois Carrq, ten miles north-east of Abbeville, on 28 October 1942 by Plt Off R A Hosking in LR424. This was the first V1 flying-bomb launching site in France to be analysed on photographs, and the buildings shown were meant for storage of flying-bomb components. Frames of Peenemünde airfield revealed a ski-type ramp pointing out to sea, which were identical to examples photographed by PR Spitfires at sites in northern France. Merrifield's photographs of the ramp went one better, for they showed a 'tiny cruciform shape set exactly on the lower end of the inclined rails – a midget aircraft actually in position for launching'.

The 'midget aircraft' was now revealed as a flying-bomb, and the curious ski-shaped ramps in France were to be the launch sites for a new reign of terror against London and southern England. The *Vergeltungswaffe* 1 (Revenge Weapon No 1), was a small, pilotless, aircraft with a 1870-lb HE warhead that detonated on impact.

On 5 December 1943 the bombing of the V1, or *Noball* sites, became part of the Operation *Crossbow* offensive. PRU aircraft regularly photographed each V1 site before and after an attack, and by the end of

The experimental rocket site at Peenemünde, photographed by a PR Mosquito after the raid, by 596 Lancasters, Halifaxes and Stirlings on 17/18 August 1943. Next morning, Flg Off R A Hosking of No 540 Sqn, in PR IX LR413, reconnoitred the target area, and returned again on 20 August (*George French*)

the month, the Allies had overflown some 42 *Noball* sites, of which 36 were revealed as having been damaged – 21 of them seriously. By 12 June 1944, 60 weapons sites had been identified. Hitler's 'rocket blitz' began on 13 June, when ten V1s, or 'Doodlebugs' as they became known, were launched against London from sites in north-eastern France.

When the enemy began building new underground storage centres in caves and quarries, vertical photography was rendered almost useless, so PR Mosquitoes in No 544 Sqn were fitted with forward-facing oblique cameras in the noses of their aircraft. Crews had to fly straight at the target at 200 ft and often brave heavy flak to obtain their photos.

By the end of September 1944, when the Allied advance overran most of the sites, 133 V1 installations had been identified by PRU aircraft. Only eight ever remained undiscovered by aerial reconnaissance.

NEW HORIZONS

Following a series of complaints from ACM Sir Arthur Harris, on 26 June 1943 No 1 PRU became No 106(PR) Wing (and from 15 May 1944, No 106 (PR) Group) at Benson. Also included in the new set up – commanded by Air Cdre J N Bootham AFC of Schneider Trophy fame – was No 309 Ferry Training and Despatch Unit, and No 8(PR) OTU at Dyce. PR Mosquito production was also at last beginning to take precedence over the bomber variant, with 90 PR IX models being ordered compared with just 54 of the B IX.

The PR IX was powered by two 1680 hp Merlin 72/73s or 76/77s, and had a fuel capacity of 860 gallons, including two 50-gal drop tanks under the wings. When it carried two 200-gal tanks, its total fuel capacity was just over 1000 gallons. Range with underwing tanks was 2450 miles at a cruising speed of 250 mph.

On 29 May 1943, No 540 Sqn received the first two PR IX Mosquitoes (LR405 and 406) off the production lines. The first sortie with the type was flown on 20 June, when Flg Off T M Clutterbuck set out to cover Zeitz and Jena in LR406, but he was forced to turn back after crossing the Dutch coast when smoke poured into the cockpit. Flg Off R A Hosking, who had taken off in LR405 soon after, had better luck, and returned with photos of the airfields at Augsburg and Oberpfaffenhofen.

On 20 August 1943, Bill White and Ron Prescott, now back at Benson, were given PR IX LR421 with which to fly their 39th op – a sortie to Bleckhammer, on the Polish border. Bill White recalls;

'Bleckhammer factories produced synthetic rubber, as Germany couldn't get a supply of natural rubber, so this was a very important target. The RAF wished to bring the wheels of the Germans to a stop due to a lack of rubber. Bleckhammer was certainly well defended. The PRU

On 29 May 1943 No 540 Sqn received the first two PR IX Mosquitoes (LR405, SoC on 1 January 1944, and LR406, which was posted missing on a mission to Danzig on 14 September 1944), and the first sortie was flown on 20 June. PR IX LR432, seen here, arrived on the squadron on 4 September 1943. A small blister on the cabin roof was a standard feature of the PR IX, although LR432 did not have one. This aircraft flew 43 sorties, the last of which was on 29 November 1944, before being passed to No 8 OTU and eventually SoC on 11 September 1945 (*via RAF Marham*)

had already flown six Mosquito ops against it and none had returned. We were to be the seventh to attempt this long trip. Ron and I took off from Benson and topped up with fuel at Coltishall. From there, we proceeded to Bleckhammer, seeing nothing more than a bit of flak. The weather was clear over the target, and we got excellent photos.

'On leaving the target, we were intercepted by fighters, and by using all our throttle power, we were able to escape from the enemy. However, when Ron calculated our fuel reserves, the strong headwinds on the route back to base meant that there was no way we would be able to make it. Our first plan was to go to Switzerland, but by conserving fuel, and helped by favourable winds, we managed to get over Yugoslavia to Naples, in Italy, before eventually running out of fuel on the west coast of Sicily. There, we made a deadstick landing at Bo Rizzo. We were unable to get 100 octane fuel, so we filled up with automobile gas.

'We got the engines started right enough, but you never heard such knocking and weird noises as came from from those Merlins. We managed to get off the ground and thumped our way over the Mediterranean to Tunis, where there was an RAF base. Having landed, the fitters changed the spark plugs and flushed out the tanks and fuel lines, and we were on our way home the next day. We refuelled at Maison Blanche, Algeria and Gibraltar, and had no further problems. All told, the trip took 14 hr 45 min.'

No 544 Sqn borrowed LR431 from the Benson pool for its first PR IX operation, which took the form of a night sortie to Vannes on 13 September 1943, flown by Flt Lt R L C Blythe . The unit received its first PR IX (LR478) on 22 October 1943, whilst the first PR IX loss occurred four days later when LR420 was posted missing. PR Mosquitoes were now very much in demand, not just for RAF bombing operations, but also by the Americans. A few weeks earlier, on 9 October 1943, 378 B-17s of the Eighth AF had been despatched on the day's operation, 115 of them going to the Arado aircraft component plant at Anklam, near Peenemünde, as a diversion for 263 bombers sent to attack the Polish port of Gydnia, and the Focke-Wulf Fw 190 factory at Marienburg.

Supporting the mission from No 540 Sqn was now Sqn Ldr R A Lenton, along with his navigator, Plt Off Heney. They took off from Leuchars to photograph Marienburg, as well as also try for Gydnia and Danzig. Just before arriving over the latter city, they were intercepted by two Bf 109s, but the Mosquito was able to escape with ease and Lenton and Heney successfully photographed the Marienburg factory. The images they brought back showed that the aircraft factory had been demolished. Lenton was subsequently reported shot down over Sylt some weeks later.

RAF PR sorties and BDA (Bomb Damage Assessment) missions were carried out on behalf of the USAAF as well as Bomber Command. After the low-level raid on the Ploesti oilfields by Liberators on 1 August 1943, BDA was provided by PR Mosquitoes from Benson on 3 and 19 August. The 2000-mile round trips revealed much damage to the refineries, which were then continually photographed by the North African PR units

Early in November 1943, Bill White and Ron Prescott were detailed to photo map the Azores, which belonged to neutral Portugal. Using PR IX LR427, they flew to Gibraltar and set off via Casablanca, arriving in the Azores on 17 November after flying through heavy rain clouds and thunderheads. Maintenance personnel and photographic specialists duly arrived in a Halifax from the UK, and the Mosquito crew carried out their task, photographing the volcanic islands. Bill White recalls;

'We were able to get the pictures with the 36-in camera. However, some islands contained active volcanoes with large clouds over them, and these had to be shot using the oblique camera. We found out that the entire islands would be free of cloud for approximately 2-3 days, every five years. I immediately wired HQ in London and asked if they wished us to remain for clear weather, which might take up to five years to arrive. Their reply next day instructed us to return to the UK! We were on our way home by 8 December. Our photos of the Azores were good, and after one more op, to Norway, Ron and I transferred to the Photo Recce OTU at Dyce. Ron and I had made 63 daylight operational flights. We had been honoured by the King, Ron being awarded the DFM and I the DFC.'

Meanwhile, on 18/19 November 1943, 'Bomber' Harris began his nightly offensive against Berlin. This series of raids, which were to last until the end of January 1944, brought added demands for bomb damage assessment (BDA). Flights over Germany were being made ever more difficult by enemy action, bad weather and other factors such as smoke from still burning factories and houses – it took no less than 31 PR Spitfire and six PR Mosquito sorties before the results of the bombing of Berlin on 18/19 November were obtained. BDA became such an issue with both the RAF and USAAF bomber commands, that PR aircraft were required to cover targets within hours of a raid being carried out – sometimes even before the returning bombers had landed.

Production of PR XVIs began in November 1943, and 435 were eventually built. With 100-gal drop tanks, the PR XVI had a range of 2000 miles. On 19 February 1944 a PR XVI brought back photos of Berlin, despite the appearance of German fighters sight ed at 42,000 ft! The first PR XVI to reach the Middle East was MM292 at the end of January 1944, and on 17 February, the first of nine PR XVIs for No 680 Sqn arrived at Matariya, Cairo – 24 hours earlier, the unit had received its first

NF II DD744 was converted to PR II standard, fitted with cameras, and painted silver. It then became one of two NF/PR IIs which joined No 60 Sqn SAAF at Castel Benito, in Tripoli, on 8 August 1943. DD744 flew the unit's first sortie, on 15 February 1944, and was SoC in November 1944

PR IX (LR444). On 7 May No 680 flew its first Mosquito PR sortie when MM333, and Flt Lt A M Yelland, covered ports and airfields in Crete and the Cyclades.

Apart from three PR IXs detached from No 540 Sqn to the Mediterranean in the summer of 1943, only a few PR Mosquitoes operated in this theatre. B Flight in No 680 Sqn mostly covered Greece and the Balkans and, later, central and southern Europe, whilst B Flight of No 60 SAAF made deep penetration sorties over southern Europe and Poland. Flt Sgt Lawrence 'Kev' Kevan, a navigator who had crewed up at No 8 OTU in December 1943 with Plt Off Ron Watson (who had already completed a PR tour on Spitfires), recalls that there were many 'highlights' and some 'hairy do's' during their tour in No 680 Sqn;

'On 26 September 1943 I flew a five-and-a-half-hour operation in MM348 with Sqn Ldr Law over Greece, the Aegean and Crete from our Forward base at Tocra, near Benghazi. I experienced my first flak (about 25 bursts) while on the photographic run up the Corinth Canal to Pireaus (Athens). It was a strange feeling lying on one's belly in the nose, giving instructions of "left-left-right-steady" etc to the pilot with those harmless looking black puff balls appearing alongside.

'On 16 October I flew another Greece-Aegean-Crete operation from Tocra, with Plt Off Ron Watson, again in MM348. On a long, curving photo run over Salonika town-harbour-railway yards, we attracted about 100 bursts, again when I was on my belly in the nose giving directions and camera operation. On landing back at Tocra, we discovered that we had sustained shrapnel hits in the forward area of the bomb-bay doors in the belly – and near mine! Four days later, in another operation to Greece and the Aegean in MM330, we flew in 10/10ths cloud with lightning for about one-and-a-half hours until, at 23,000 ft, Ron decided that it was mission impossible and he was beginning to disbelieve his instruments.

PR XVI NS705 is seen in flight over England with its port airscrew feathered for the benefit of the camera (*via Mrs P Wood*)

He dived immediately, and we finally broke cloud at about 1000 ft above the Corinth Canal. We remained at almost sea level back across the Med to Tocra. I think that we were extremely lucky.

'On 29 October it was off again in MM330 from Tocra to Greece-Salonika-Crete, which we had to abandon when, south of Athens, Ron had to feather the starboard engine after he could not control the revs. We made an emergency landing at Hassani (Athens), where the groundcrew found that a nut on the CSU had stripped. After a good night in Athens (the Greeks treated us as though we were Gods descended from Mount Olympus!), we returned to Tocra on 30 October, and on 1 November, in MM330 again, we set out on the operation we had abandoned.

'However, we only got as far as Crete when we had to feather the starboard engine yet again! We went on to IFF and made a successful S/E landing at Tocra. All went well on 22 November, in MM297, to Rhodes-Dodeconese-Melos-Crete, but we attracted 50 accurate flak bursts on a run over Suda Bay. September, October and November 1944 had been quite an exciting time for Ron and myself.'

Meanwhile, in the UK, the first PR XVI production examples had been urgently despatched to No 140 Sqn, 2nd Tactical Air Force (TAF), at Hartford Bridge, where they supplemented PR IXs on recce and mapping duties – part of the build up to D-Day. No 544 Sqn began receiving PR XVIs in March 1944, while No 540 had to wait until July.

2nd TAF decided that rather than have all its fighter units flying tactical reconnaissance, its three recce Wings should each contain a PR unit. B Flight of No 4 Sqn in No 35 Wing (84 Group) and A Flight of No 400 Sqn RCAF in No 39 Wing (83 Group) therefore received PR XVIs for the role. At the end of May 1944 both flights reverted back to Spitfire IXs, but No 140 Sqn, operating in No 34 PR Wing (HQ), retained all its PR XVIs, which they had equipped with *Gee* and *Rebecca* so as to fly long-range blind night photography operations, first from Northolt, and later, the continent. Flg Off Arthur T Kirk, a pilot in No 140 Sqn, recalls;

'At the end of July 1944, Sgt Mike Pedder – my navigator – and I, set off on our first trip over France. Our target was a stretch of country between Grand Courronne and Hautot. The excitement got to Mike a bit, and he kept looking round behind. I said, "Look Mike, I've been on nightfighters, and it's no good you looking round behind. If there's anything up our rear end, we'll know about it soon enough!" It did the trick

PR 32 NS589 at Hatfield in October 1944, shortly before it joined No 540 Sqn. Five aircraft, all of which started as PR XVIs, were completed as PR 32s, fitted with a pressure cabin and specially lightened, and lengthened, wingtips. The first flew in August 1944. The PR 32 could reach 42,000 ft, and its two-stage 1690 hp Merlin 113 (starboard)/114 (port) engines added an extra 30 mph to the top speed. NS589 was the first PR 32 used operationally, on 5 December 1944, when Wg Cdr A H W 'Freddie' Ball DSO, DFC (later AM Sir Arthur) and Flt Lt E G Leatham DFC photographed Darmstadt and Mannheim – during the sortie they were intercepted by two Luftwaffe fighters. In its 14 operations, NS589 was used exclusively to photograph the German railway network, and on 14 March 1945 brought back photos which showed that 100 yards of the Bielefeld viaduct had collapsed through the 'earthquake effect' of the 22,000 lb 'Grand Slam' and 'Tallboy' bombs dropped by No 617 Sqn (*via Philip Jarrett*)

Nine PR XVIs were initially issued to No 680 Sqn at Matariya, in Cairo, in early 1944. The unit flew its first Mosquito PR sortie on 7 May 1944 ('Kev' Kevan Collection)

and we settled into the task. On our second op we photographed the road between Thury-Harcourt and Caen, as our troops were bogged down and needed information about opposing forces.

'The third trip was to the Falaise area, which was soon to be a scene of bloody carnage as German armour was caught and savaged by rocket-firing Typhoons and other fighter-bombers. We returned to find our cameras had obtained only three photographs instead of the dozen expected from each camera. It appeared that this had occurred on all of our sorties so far as, somehow, we had got the camera programming sequence wrong. After a sort-out, we did a lot better.'

In August 1944 67 of No 140 Sqn's long-range mapping sorties were at night. Arthur Kirk again;

'We carried out three night operations, two of them along the River Orne, and another from Barentin to Pavilly, when we saw Rouen under the shellfire. Mike navigated using *Gee*, sometimes *Rebecca*, or even *Oboe*. We carried 12 flashes in the belly of the Mossie, and as they were released, they exploded at the set height, operating the camera shutters by photo-electric cells. On a good op we got 24 pictures of troops, trucks, trains and armoured columns. Sometimes we'd be sent to photograph river crossings supposedly in use by the Wehrmacht – anything the Army wanted to know about movement in the area, or was considered important to the overall strategy, we photographed. We plotted our track to enter France unnoticed if possible, with Fecamp, on the coast, being a favourite landfall. The "natives" didn't seem to be too unfriendly there!

'Occasionally, we would be frustrated by jamming, or on-board malfunctions, and we had to rely on more basic techniques: dead reckon-

Les Deadfield, a ground crewman in No 60 Sqn SAAF, poses in front of BANCVIRNLES at San Severo, Italy, in 1944 (Les Deadfield via Theo Boiten)

ing, or map-reading, if conditions allowed. We were not the only air-craft inhabiting the night sky, and sometimes we would see Bomber Command unloading their deadly cargoes, from the target indicators, splashes of vivid reds, greens or yellows saturating the aiming points, followed by exploding bombs, flak and searchlights probing until they lit one or more of the bombers like a moth in a candle-glow. Once or twice we saw them pounced on by all and sundry and, amid the flashes, streams of tracer and billowing smoke, catching fire. We always

PR XVI MM386 of No 60 Sqn SAAF
(*via Philip Jarrett*)

An airstrip in Greece, photographed
on 13 October 1944 by Ron Watson
and 'Kev' Kevan of No 680 Sqn.
Ju 52 transports have been marked
by the Photo Interpretation Unit
(*'Kev' Kevan Collection*)

looked for parachutes and hoped they all got out. On night reconnaissance we didn't lose a crew, or have one injured, while I was with the unit, although aircraft did suffer damage through flak. The Mosquito was an elusive bird, even more so at night!'

No 140 Sqn provided photo coverage throughout the winter of 1944-45, moving to France in September to keep in touch with the action. In January 1945, Flt Lt Kirk got a new navigator, Flt Lt Anthony Guy Humphryes, who was the unit's navigation leader. Kirk recalls;

'We did 17 operations together. Our best joint effort was on the night of 24 February, when were were sent to photograph the railway sidings at München Gladbach. We approached the target three times. Each time, just as we were set to release the flashes, the "natives" were decidedly hostile. Lots of little red balls kept coming up at us, starting off apparently quite slowly, then, as they got nearer, whizzing very rapidly by. I didn't think we'd get very good pictures while all this was going on. We had a moment's consultation as to how best to cope with the situation.

'I decided to do the run in reverse. I asked Tony to navigate us to the far end of the run and give me a reciprocal course to steer. He put his skills to work, and at the correct moment we turned onto the target, straightened up, and raced over the marshalling yard. Down went the flashes one after another, going off like bolts of summer lightning. We didn't mind the gunners shooting at our tail as we left – perhaps the million candle-power flashes put them off a bit! Next morning, the photos delighted the interpreters, as well as Tony and I. This night, added to our other efforts, earned us a DFC each.'

Meanwhile, since just before D-Day, No 544 Sqn had flown special rail sorties in daylight to France in an effort to detect any movement of Panzers towards the Normandy beachhead as early as possible. If any movement was observed, the crew had to land at Farnborough to give a verbal report to SHEAF HQ, who would then initiate interdiction bombing by 2nd TAF medium bombers. On 3 June 1944, Flt Lt Alan 'Joe' Morgan and Sgt Frank 'Ginger' Baylis flew the first No 544 Sqn 'rail recce' to cover lines

PR XV1 NS644/G of No 680 Sqn in flight (*David Cox Collection*)

between Mont de Marsan and Bordeaux. Baylis recalls;

'We spent about an hour in the area, which made Joe quite uncomfortable, as the last time he flew over Merignac in 1941, he'd had a pasting with accurate flak. Our most memorable "railway recce" was on 6 August. We had been briefed to follow the railway from south of Paris to Lyon, then up towards Belfort. As we trundled towards Lyon, we saw this huge smoke cloud rising to 20,000 ft from oil tanks south of the town. We could even see flames from our height of 28,000 ft.

'Conjecturing that "it must be a raid by Fifteenth AF heavy bombers from Italy" (there had been no information given at briefing), we cut across to the rail line leading NE to Belfort. As Joe turned quite steeply, I took an instant shot of the fire and towering smoke. We settled onto the railway, and Joe asked me to have a last look around. Good job. I saw 12 fighters in three groups of four obviously in hot pursuit. At my urging, Joe put the throttles through the "gate", and we managed to avoid them, aided by some high thunderheads in which we played "hide and seek" for ten minutes or so.'

On 27 August 1944, one of the longest PR flights was flown by No 540 Sqn's CO, Wg Cdr J R H Merrifield DSO, DFC, in a PR XVI. Taking off from Benson at 0600 hours, he photographed Gydnia, Danzig, Konigsberg and Bromberg, in Poland, Gleiwitz, in south-eastern Germany, and oil installations at Bleckhammer, Bratislava and Zarsa, on the Dalmatian coast, before landing at San Severo, Italy, at 1210 hours. After refuelling, the Mosquito took off again at 1500 hours to make the return flight to Benson, where it landed at 1900 hours, having photographed Pola, Trieste, Millstadt, in the Tyrol, and Le Havre on the return leg.

PR operations to northern Norway, meanwhile (especially those concerned with maintaining a watchful eye on the *Tirpitz),* were not being neglected, for the No 544 Sqn detachment at Leuchars was kept constantly busy. In March 1944 *Tirpitz* had left its anchorage in Alten Fjord, and later that month was found in Kaa Fjord by a PRU Spitfire of No 542 Sqn, operating from Russia. On 3 April the ship was damaged in an attack by RN aircraft from *Victorious* and *Furious*, but to what extent, no one knew. Flt Sgt Eric Hill, a navigator in No 544 Sqn, recalls;

'The operational task was to carry out a visual and PR of the west coast of Norway, flying as far north as fuel permitted, and certainly beyond the Lofoten Islands, paying attention to any fjords likely to provide suitable anchorage for the *Tirpitz*. Due to a rare gap in intelligence, there was great uncertainty as to her location and readiness for action – she was always a potential threat to Atlantic shipping and Murmansk-bound convoys.'

On 9 July 1944, Eric Hill and his pilot, Flt Lt Frank L Dodd (in PR XVI NS504), carried out a search for the elusive 45,000-ton battleship at heights ranging from between 6000 and 24,000 ft over the Norwegian shipping lanes from Stetlandet to the Lofoten Islands, including Narvik. NS504 was hit by flak in the starboard wing whilst photographing Bodø at 15,000 ft. Nevertheless, valuable negative information was obtained

from this sortie, the Mosquito having been airborne 7hr 44 min when it landed back at Leuchars with less than ten gallons of petrol remaining.

On 12 July Dodd and Hill flew NS504 to Sumburgh to top up their tanks for another sortie in search of the *Tirpitz*. Hill recalls;

'We had to operate with petrol overload (the numbing 100-gal wing tanks, which were relatively untried at the time) at extreme range, with the weather on return likely to irretrievably clamp down most of the northern British airfields. There were other hazards too, apart from the fact that Sumburgh was a small drome, with one runway, usually crosswind, and demanding a steepish turn to avoid a hill near the town. Frank handled this beautifully as always – even then, with a full fuel load, tail-wheel and chimney pots were too close for comfort as we climbed away. We set off, with me still wondering why our dear allies, the Russians, would not let us land at Murmansk to refuel, thus making the job about 400 per cent more likely to succeed, and what had happened to the glorious Norwegian underground, who were supposed to be keeping an eye on the battleship?

Above and top
PR XVI NS502/M was delivered to No 544 Sqn on 23 May 1944 and operated over Europe until 21 February 1945, when it crashed. After repair, this aircraft served with the Royal Navy at RNAS Fleetlands from 7 November 1947 (*via Philip Jarrett*)

On 4 September 1944 Flt Lt Ken W Watson RAAF (top) and Flg Off Ken H Pickup RAFVR (bottom) of No 540 Sqn were flying PR IX LR429 when they were attacked over Nürnburg at 29,000 ft by Me 262s. For 15 minutes they evaded them, before escaping at 1500 ft, but not before hitting the tip of a Bavarian pine tree, which shattered the nose perspex and filled the cockpit with pine needles, making it very cold, uncomfortable and draughty. The pair flew on through the Brenner Pass to San Severo, Italy, where they safely recovered. After repairs, LR429 was written off the next day in a crashlanding after the crew tried to return to Benson. Both men were unhurt, and they completed their tours. Watson was killed landing an RAF Canberra on 3 June 1954 when a Night Photo Flash bomb exploded in the bomb-bay following a test flight to Cuxhaven (*Pickup Collection*)

'Fortunately, the weather for the first part of the sortie was reasonable, and we were able to start the recce at 25,000 ft with out any apparent hostility. However, when 15 miles west of Bodø, we were greeted by a perfect box-barrage of flak at our precise height, which set the adrenaline flowing. This was just as well, because we needed all our wits about us shortly afterwards when the weather deteriorated, necessitating a blind Dead Reckoning descent through heavy cloud to regain visual contact, as we approached where we estimated the Lofoten islands to be. Happily, the D/R navigation turned out to be correct and there were no hard centres to the clouds. Unfortunately, still no sign of the *Tirpitz*, so no alternative but to press on to Alten Fjord, which intelligence thought might be a possible lair.

'We gentled up the coast and started to sneak into the many fjords past the Lofotens, until we came to Alten. Our relatively low height (we were at an uncomfortable 8000 ft under the cloud, in an essentially high level kite) had apparently worked in our favour as far as tactical surprise was concerned, for as we cleared the hills before the fjord we saw the *Tirpitz*, naked without a smokescreen, looking oddly menacing and peaceful at the same time.

'A bit of desultory flak down the fjord persuaded Frank to steep turn on to a short photographic run on the ship. Almost immediately, there was a huge explosion, maps, Q codes, escape kits, Horlicks tablets, hopes and fears, flew wildly around the cabin and I thought, "God, these Germans are bloody good". They weren't. The top of the cabin had just flown off into the fjord. Anxiously. we checked that we were OK, then noted with surprised relief that so was the kite, apart from the top.

'We did the run, Frank calmly keeping me paying attention, then set off for a very long, chilly, anxious, noisy, frustrating, 1000 mile, four-hour trip back in a damaged aircraft, with a vast question mark over landing conditions. A petrol twitch and – what I was to find a lot later – the fact that nobody would talk to us on W/T or R/T because all the codes, which changed frequently, had gone out the top into the 'oggin of Alten Fjord. I put some outrageous priorities on my W/T requests for courses to steer and aerodromes to land at. Once I told them our unit, aircraft num-

ber and service numbers in order to establish who we were, but to no avail.

'We discussed feathering one engine as the fuel situation was getting desperate. In our crippled condition we had to keep away from the enemy, and fly at 15,000 ft because of the fuel position – our most vulnerable height. The sea, what we could see of it through generally 10/10ths cloud, looked unusually calm for the North Sea, suggesting that the light winds I had found on the way up, had, crucially, not changed.

'At long, long last, we saw a gap in the cloud just after ETA, dived anxiously through it, and saw land. Soon it became Wick, the most northerly mainland drome there, and with all the fuel gauges reading zero, Frank made the most treasured landing of all. We had spent 7hr 45 min in the air, having covered an air distance of about 2300 miles, with Frank's careful course keeping and cosseting of the engines a vital factor in our survival and in getting some useful gen. On landing at Wick, the aircraft was immediately refuelled, and we flew down to make a night landing at Leuchars, after a total flying time for the whole sortie, of 9 hr 25 min.'

For this outstanding operation Flt Lt (later AVM) Dodd was awarded an immediate DSO. In September, Flt Sgt (later Flg Off) Hill was awarded the DFM.

The *Tirpitz* would have to be put out of action once and for all by Lancasters of No 5 Group. On 11 September 1944, 38 Lancasters of Nos 9 and 617 Sqns, accompanied by Flt Lt George Watson and Wt Off John McArthur in PR XVI MM397 to provide up-to-date target information and weather reports, flew to their forward base at Archangel, in northern Russia. The attack, by 27 Lancasters – 20 of which were carrying 'Tallboys', the others, 400-500 lb 'Johnny Walker 'mines' – went ahead on 15 September, and considerable damage was caused to the battleship. Subsequent PR revealed that although badly damaged, the *Tirpitz* was still afloat (albeit beyond practical repair, although this was not known at the time). The next

A Wellington XIII of No 69 Sqn, Spitfire PR XI of No 16 Sqn and a PR XVI Mosquito of No 140 Sqn are parked together at Melsbroek, in Belgium, in March 1945. All were from No 34 (PR) Wing, 2nd TAF (*Flight*)

Flt Sgt Eric Hill (third from left) was a navigator in No 544 Sqn, and he is seen here with his pilot, Flt Lt Frank L Dodd (extreme right), Wg Cdr A H W 'Freddie' Ball DSO, DFC (later AM Sir Arthur) and fellow wartime navigator, Ronnie Knight (extreme left) (*Eric Hill Collection*)

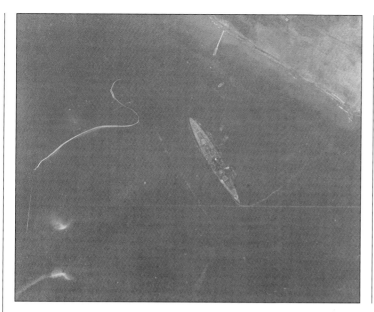

The *Tirpitz* photographed from 15,000 ft by Flt Lt Sandy Powell and Flt Sgt Joe Townshend of No 540 Sqn in PR XVI NS641 on 18 October 1944. The main purpose of the flight was to establish where the battleship had moved to, so therefore there was no need to go much below the cloud base. The position of the ship was 260°, 3³/₄ miles to the west of Tromsø – exactly the same spot it was sunk in by Lancasters on 12 November (*Joe Townshend*)

day, Flt Lt Frank Dodd and Flt Sgt Eric Hill had a most harrowing trip, as the latter recalls;

'Having got what we hoped were some decent pictures of the oilworks at Magdeburg, we spotted two of the new Me 262s, and were chased around for what seemed an age. When I gave the order to turn, Frank flung old NS639 into some violent turns, unnerving them as they skidded by, unable to hold our turn. About eight times it happened. At one time Frank frightened the daylights out of them by lining up behind them for an imaginary squirt with our non-existent guns. Frank found some cloud, into which we gratefully disappeared.

'After a quiet spell trying to confuse the radar, we emerged, hoping to be able to head for home. Flak came up a little off our port wing while the two jets were perched about 100 yards away on the starboard and above. This could have been nasty, but we found some more cloud, played possum for long enough this time, and trolleyed home, happy to hear Benson's call-sign "Gingerwine", welcoming us into the fold.'

On 17 October 1944 a detachment of four PR Mosquitoes from No 540 Sqn was despatched to Dyce to keep watch on *Tirpitz*. Information from the Norwegian resistance stated that the ship had left Kaa Fjord on its way south for Tromsø, where it was to be used as a heavy artillery battery. On 18 October, Flt Lt Hubert C S 'Sandy' Powell and Flt Sgt Joe Townshend set out in PR XVI NS641 to investigate. Townshend recalls;

On 22 March 1945, Sqn Ldr Frank L Dodd and Plt Off Eric Hill flew a ten-and-a-half-hour round trip to Norway, where they photographed the *Tirpitz* lying capsized in Tromsø fjord (*via Eddie Leaf*)

Sgt Frank Baylis and his pilot, Flt Lt O M 'Danny' Daniels, of No 544 Sqn. Baylis had already completed 46 PR sorties with Flt Lt Morgan in No 544 Sqn between January and October 1944 before crewing up with Daniels on No 54(M) PR Course at No 8 PR OTU at Dyce. They flew their first operation together on 5 December 1944 in PR XVI NS696 while still on the course. Baylis finished the war having completed 63 trips and 300 operational hours (*Baylis Collection*)

'We took off from Dyce on our 25th trip, and 55 minutes later we landed at Scatsta (now Sullom Voe) in North Shetland in order to top up with fuel. In the air again at 0940, we set course for Norway. On switching from inner to outer tanks, we soon found that one of the 97-gal drop tanks was not feeding, leaving 763 gallons for a flight of some 1600 miles over the sea. There would be little margin. We climbed to 25,000 ft, first saw rocks at 1130, and then followed the coast north, searching every fjord. We were over Bodø at 1152, and at 1230 we saw the *Tirpitz*, 3³⁄₄ miles to the west of Tromsø, 215 miles inside the Arctic Circle. By this time we had come down to 15,000 ft due to cloud, and we made one photographic run over the ship at 15,000 ft. There was some firing from the *Tirpitz* and the ground, but it was not accurate.

'We left for home immediately, and on the return journey, heading into wind, Sandy was again intent on nursing the engines for maximum performance from minimum fuel consumption. Wind lanes and "white horses" on the sea indicated that the wind had changed little, and at 1355 I tried to get a long-range fix. The position given was ignored as it was well to the west of our course, and probably came from a German station in Norway. At 1423 a QTE Sumburgh 032° confirmed we were on course. We later obtained two fixes and, finally, a QDM Sumburgh 220°. Two tired crew landed at Scatsta at 1616, with 15 minutes' fuel left. We were back at Dyce at 1800 after 2150 miles in an overall 8 hr 35 min flying.'

Their outstanding feat earned Powell a DFC and Townshend the DFM. Teamwork, once again, had played a huge part in the success of these operations. Sandy Powell recalls;

'Joe Townshend's phlegmatic attitude to enemy belligerence, coupled with a keen intelligence and outstanding navigational abilities, was the driving force that enabled us to survive over 50 sorties. Imagine being in an aircraft, at 20-30,000 ft, centred in an open sky, in daylight, hundreds of miles inside enemy territory. You are aware of being fully exposed, and know you've been detected by enemy radar since you crossed the coast, and every mile since then. Around you, an implacable enemy watches, waits and could at any moment, range its mighty forces against you.

'You think of several targets you've been briefed to photograph, and those leagues of hostile country that need to be traversed in order to carry out your mission. Then how long you must spend in hostile space before getting back home. If you can truly imagine all this, then you become aware of what it is like to feel truly lonely. Someone once said, "PRU was the loneliest job in the world". There are rewards, however, when you return over the shores of the UK. Adrenaline charges through your being, and you become a giant, ten feet tall.'

Lancasters finally capsized the *Tirpitz* on 12 November 1944, and about one-and-a-half hours later, Flt Lt A R Cussons and Flt Sgt Ken Ellis from No 540 Sqn took photos which showed the ship had indeed 'turned turtle'. Meanwhile, in addition to the detachment at Yagodnik, in the USSR, covering the No 5 Group operations against the *Tirpitz*, a detachment from No 540 Sqn had also been established at Gibraltar in September in preparation for a survey of the Canary Islands.

Further trips to the USSR commenced on 9 October with courier flights for Operation *Frugal* – No 544 Sqn's Mosquitoes transited to the Soviet Union, via Memel, to Ramenskoye for eventual operations over

Aalborg town photographed on 5 January 1945 by Flt Lt 'Danny' Daniels and Sgt Frank Baylis in PR XVI MM307. The freezing cold has caused the effect of static sparking across the film as it wound on between exposures (*Baylis Collection*)

eastern Germany and Poland. These flights lasted six hours, and when Moscow (Vnukovo) was used, they became 4hr 30 min trips for the crews involved. Others were flown to Yalta, via San Severo, in Italy, and Saki, in the Crimea, or via Malta and Cairo. In December, some Mosquitoes were stripped of their cameras and used to carry diplomatic mail to Hassani, in Greece – this run, known as Operation *Haycock*, was extended to Italy and Egypt in connection with the Cairo Conference. A similar service was performed by the PR Mosquitoes during the Potsdam Conference.

Late in 1944 Flt Sgt Frank Baylis crewed up with Flt Lt O M Daniels on No 54(M) PR Course at 8 PR OTU at Dyce. Baylis recalls;

'Danny was a gritty Canadian from Windsor, Ontario. A skilful pilot, you might say he was a born flyer. Good job. His ability was tested to the utmost on 5 December 1944 when we did a sortie from Dyce to Norway in a "brand new" PR XVI (NS696). We lost our hydraulic fluid on the starboard prop, and suffered an overspeeding engine at 28,000 ft, about

Navigator Flt Lt C R 'Mickey' Randles (left) and his pilot, Flt Lt Guy Trevor, of No 540 Sqn, 104 Wing at Coulommiers, France in April 1945. On 13 December 1945, at the end of an air test in PR 34 RG228, the starboard engine first cut and over-revved at 28,000 ft over France and again, as they returned, over Beachy Head at 4000 ft. They attempted to land at RNAS Ford, but lost height alarmingly, and crashed 400 yards southeast of Ford railway station. After being knocked out, Randles came to in the wreckage on the River Arun. Guy Trevor had drowned (*C R Randles Collection*)

30 ml N of Bergen. We operated the Graviner, which put the fire out, then the engine broke up, and the resulting 12-ft diameter "circle" stuck on the leading edge of the starboard wing rendered our aircraft quite unable to remain airworthy.

'By the time I was ready to bail out, we were down to 7000 ft, and Danny said he thought he could hold her before we reached the briny, and would I like to stay? Not half. A dip in Norwegian coastal waters in mid-December did not appeal, so I returned to my seat. With both feet holding the rudder-bar at its fullest extension, Danny wrestled NS696 all the way back to Sumburgh, where he managed a good single-engined landing. Much relief all round. Danny had flown 1hr 20 min at about 140 mph – just above stalling speed.'

Daniels and Baylis joined B Flight of No 544 Sqn at Benson, and flew their first squadron operation on New Year's Day, to Denmark.

A few days earlier, on 23 December, No 544 Sqn's Frank Dodd and Eric Hill had experienced an eventful first sortie in PR 32 NS587 to Magdeburg. They distrusted the PR 32 – 'a very high flyer, but unreliable', recalls Hill. NS587 had been tested thoroughly in November, during which time it had earned a bad reputation due to engines overheating and myriad other problems manifesting themselves. In the event, this aircraft became the only PR 32 allotted to No 544 Sqn;

'We had "done" a few targets, plus the oilworks, when suddenly a horrifying mixture of impedimenta poured out of the starboard engine, which Frank hastily feathered. Now, being over the Third Reich with a crippled, unarmed, Mossie at 41,000 ft, making a huge, persistent, contrail in a completely cloudless sky, was decidedly suggesting a desire to end it all. I knocked out a course for the nearest bit of the North Sea. Frank went into a fastish dive, and I was kneeling on the seat as usual looking anxiously backwards. In due course, somewhere near Emden, I yelled frantically, "Fighter, my side, above, closing fast!"

'Despite the fact that the Fw 190 was superior in the climb, the dive, the turn and short-speed bursts than we were, provided you saw a fighter early enough, and had a decent Mossie (they varied like cars), you could get away eventually by maintaining straight and level top speed. We knew, too, that if you managed to lose a fighter once, the sky is a big enough space to give you a good chance of getting away.

'My world turned upside down. Frank flung the kite into a vertical dive, which clearly took the Fw 190 pilot by surprise, as when I was able to examine his bit of sky again, he was diving disgustedly earthwards. My joy at losing him soon evaporated. Frank's dive had started up the u/s engine, which now screamed and howled and shook the kite as if it was just going to depart and leave us in bits. Frank pulled her up into a near stall, rapidly pushed the feathering button and, like me, I reckon he prayed. It worked, for the engine stopped. We found a nice quiet bit of German coast, and in a fast dive, worked our way home.

'The weather in England was poor, but when out of range of the German jammers, I was able to use the *Gee* set to get us right into dear old Benson on a brilliant system worked out by Flt Lt "Lofty" South – a huge chap with a fine brain, who had been a policeman, and who taught us how to tell pilots not only what course to steer, but when to change pitch, put down wheels and flaps, and when to hold off. Hearing that we were coming back on one engine, half of Benson – all the aircrew, all the blood wagons and fire engines – turned out to watch the fun. A perfect three-pointer on one engine was vintage Dodd.'

'Lofty' South and his pilot, Flg Off R M Hays, later had a harrowing flight in PR XVI NS795 on 16 March 1945 when, over Leipzig, they were intercepted by three Me 163 rocket-powered fighters. Hays managed to throw them off by putting the Mosquito into a 480 mph dive, during which the starboard engine caught fire. After feathering the propeller the fire went out, so they decided to set course for the Allied lines. Flying through violent frontal conditions, they were then jumped by a Bf 109, which Hays threw off once again by putting the nose down and diving for the ground, before pulling up. NS795 eventually landed at Lille, still on one engine. For this exploit, Hays was awarded an immediate DFC. Two weeks later, on 30 March, Hays and South were killed when they lost an engine on take-off from Benson.

On 30 April 1945, navigator Lawrence 'Kev' Kevan, who was now a warrant officer in No 680 Sqn at Deversoir, in the Egyptian canal zone, endured an even more harrowing experience. He and Ron Watson, now a flying officer, were set for an operation which would complete their tour. Just before take-off time, the original flight plan was scrubbed because HQ ME wanted an urgent low level visual recce of a suspected radar site on Rhodes. Kevan recalls;

'At 0820 we were airborne in MM333. After a visual recce of the islands of Allinia and Calchi (off the western coast of Rhodes) at about 1000 ft, we headed for the radar site somewhere near Kattavia airfield, on the southern tip of Rhodes. We came down to 200 ft, and in a small clearing among trees was a radar mast. Ron took the plane down to about 30 ft so that I could get as much detail as possible. There appeared to be no Germans around, so Ron decided to repeat the run at 30 ft to make sure that we had not missed anything. Suddenly, as we approached head-on, soldiers firing

PR XVI in No 540 Sqn, 104 Wing at Coulommiers, France in April 1945. Note the unpainted metal spinners (*C R Randles Collection*)

35

Wt Off 'Kev' Kevan of No 680 Sqn
(*'Kev' Kevan Collection*)

automatic guns appeared. The aircraft was badly hit, and so were we.

'He hauled back the controls and up we zoomed. I thought, "Good, he's OK". At level-off at about 1500 ft however, Ron suddenly said, "Take the controls, Kev", which I did, but thought he would take back control. However, when he tried to he could not. His next words shook me. "Take it home Kev and prang it! I can't move". He left me holding the control column. I had never had a flying lesson! Furthermore, in the confirmed space of a Mossie cockpit, there was no way in which we could change seats, especially with an unconscious and wounded pilot. Thoughts were racing through my head, and I decided to lift Ron's feet off the rudder bar, hold the aircraft at about 1500 ft, and head towards the sun, which should fetch me up on the Egyptian coast (i.e., southwards).

'After a while Ron came to and asked, "Why are we heading south – go for Crete, it's nearer". I said no, we would not stand any chance in the mountains. He drifted into unconsciousness again and I struggled on for another half an hour or so, when he again came to and quietly said, "Kev, I'm going – say goodbye to my folks for me". I told him not to talk like that. We would get through somehow. However, Ron was sure he was dying, and told me to shake hands and say goodbye. To comfort him, I did, and he sank back into an unconscious state.

'I now started using the pilot's R/T to make people aware of my situation, and also switched the IFF on to "Mayday". Having to bend over Ron's legs and reach down to the R/T controls on his left was not easy, and caused quite a switchback ride for the aircraft. After many attempts, I finally heard Lydda control calling "Cleveland 25" – my call sign! They advised me to turn on to a course of 090°, and head for the coast of Palestine, which I eventually reached.

'Lydda then started asking all sorts of technical details about the aircraft, and about landing. When I replied that "I was the navigator and had never landed an aircraft", there was a stunned silence. Their advice was to bale out, but I believed my pilot still had a chance, so I told them I must try and land. I could not operate the R/T and fly the aircraft, so I told them I would not be talking any more, but for them to keep speaking to me. They replied, "OK – Good Luck".

'I reduced height and approached what I thought was Lydda airfield, but then I found out that I was over Petah Tiqva airfield to the east of Tel Aviv, and so I had to refind Lydda. BIG problems came to the fore in the circuit. I had no rudder control, and I was flying from the navigator's position. The aircraft was trimmed for flying and at 250-300 mph, and I dare not play about with the throttles or use flaps, and certainly not attempt a wheels-down landing! After three circuits, where, on each attempt to line up on Runway 28, I could not get the aircraft lower than about 20 ft, and I had to open up and go around again.

'On the final go I had decided "Now or never", and forced the aircraft down onto the runway at about 200 mph! Thankfully, I touched down level on both engine nacelles. The impact, which took most of the propellers and gears off, was so great that the aircraft took off again and rose several hundred feet. I kept her level and flattened out at the top of the rise, and knew that I had to get her down again on a level keel – any poor judgement now would be fatal!

'I pushed the control column gently forward and then back when I judged that I was near the ground. I was out of runway now and finally landed in fields beyond, rushing along on the Mossie's belly at a rate of knots! I saw a peasant with his donkey standing transfixed right in my path. I yanked the column to port and the aircraft turned through 90° and stopped. Great red clouds shot up all round. "God!" I thought, we are on fire. No, it was the red earth that had been disturbed.

'I released my harness and Ron's. I tried to lift him but could not move him. I jumped on to the wing and saw the ambulance, fire engine and station wagon rushing across the fields. The station group captain helped me done, and both Ron and I were taken in the ambulance to hospital, where my arm wound was dressed. Later that evening I was told that Ron had died on the flight home. We had been hit by Dum-Dum bullets, and Ron had been hit in the stomach and would never have survived.

'Thus ended our tour and 16 months of flying together. This last flight had lasted 5 hr 40 min, and I had flown MM333 for 2 hr 40 min. The next day, Ron was buried in Ramla cemetery, and his funeral was attended by No 680 Sqn officers and AM Sir Charles Medhurst (AOC in C ME). After the burial, with the RAF guard of honour formed up, AM Medhurst awarded me an immediate DFC at Ron's grave side.'

Navigator, Plt Off Eric Hill in No 544 Sqn concludes;

'Flying solitary missions over heavily-defended enemy territory in unarmed wooden aircraft I suppose needed special qualities. After it all, I had the best luck of all. I had Frank Dodd as a pilot, whose brilliant airmanship, calm appreciations and simple courage got us through. Perhaps many other navigators will say the same of their pilots, and just to end this tribute to them all, I hope that many who have forgotten the part PRU played in the victory, will perhaps pause and reconsider.'

Flg Off Ron Watson was a pilot with No 680 Sqn, and he is seen in front of MM333 – the same Mosquito used on the squadron's first sortie on 7 May 1944, and in which he and 'Kev' Kevan flew their last op together on 30 April 1945 (*'Kev' Kevan Collection*)

STARS AND STRIPES

On 20 April 1941 Maj Gen Hap Arnold, Chief of the USAAC, Maj Elwood Quesda, General Arnold's aide, and later to control IX Fighter Command in England, and other senior officers, were present at Hatfield when the Mosquito prototype (W4050), in the hands of Geoffrey de Havilland Jr, was demonstrated to Lord Beaverbrook, Minister of Aircraft Production. The Americans were greatly impressed by the Mosquito's performance, and had long been interested in setting up production in Canada and Australia. However, in America, the Material Division of the AAC placed little importance in the Mosquito, expecting that the F-4 (P-38) Lightning would be capable of carrying out US PR needs.

In the summer of 1942, Col Elliott Roosevelt brought two squadrons of F-4 Lightnings and a squadron of B-17F 'mapping Fortresses' to Britain. The President's son was preparing his 3rd PR Group for the invasion of North Africa in November (Operation *Torch*), and was to work with the RAF until considered operationally ready. Given a B IV Mosquito for combat evaluation, Roosevelt discovered that the Mosquito outperformed his F-4s, and had five times the range. Gen Hap Arnold wanted 200 Mosquitoes to equip all American PR squadrons in Europe, and in October 1943 Britain agreed to supply 120 to the USAAF for reconnaissance. Ultimately, however, only 34 F 8s (converted from B XXs) and six F-8-DHs (converted from Canadian B VIIs) ever reached the USAAF. These aircraft were to prove very unpopular with the AAF in

Ex-RAF PR XVI NS619, still in its overall PRU blue paint scheme, is seen at its dispersal at Watton. 25th BG PR XVIs were used on all manner of weather-reconnaissance, spying and PR missions by the 653rd and 654th BSs (*via Ron MacKay*)

England and all (except 11 which were returned to the RAF in late 1944 and early 1945) eventually went to the 3rd PRG in the MTO

Planning for Operation *Husky* – the invasion of Sicily – began in November 1942, and two PR Mosquitoes from No 544 Sqn were loaned to Roosevelt's PR group at Algiers in December for the duration. In February 1943 Gen Carl Spaatz asked that two PR Mosquitoes be lent to Gen Eisenhower, and two were duly borrowed from the No 540 Sqn detachment at Gibraltar, but despite repeated pleas, were never returned! They were retained in North Africa throughout the winter of 1943, one subsequently crashing – it was not replaced owing to a lack of spares.

In March 1943 No 680 Sqn and the US 3rd PRG formed the North African PR Wing, under the unified command of Col Elliot Roosevelt. In April Gen Arnold requested PR Mosquitoes for special tasks, but was told that insufficient aircraft were available. AM Tedder pointed out that Mosquitoes were required for urgent mapping operations, and that only aircraft fitted with 36-in cameras could undertake the task. Two more PR Mosquitoes subsequently arrived to join No 3 PRG.

For a time the USAAF had to persist with F-5-mapping Lightnings and F-6s (modified P-51s). By March 1944, when American production lines were producing enough PR aircraft for the USAAF, the Mediterranean Theatre of Operations (MTO) cancelled its requirement for the Mosquito, choosing to standardise on the F-5 intead. In England, meanwhile, the Eighth AF had one reconnaissance group equipped with F-5s and Spitfires, while the Ninth AF had three groups. Rather than replace any of these aircraft, the decision was taken to organise a group within the Eighth using Mosquitoes, and on 22 April 1944 the 802nd Reconnaissance Group (P) was formed at Watton, in Norfolk, comprising the 652nd Heavy Weather Sqn, equipped with the B-17 and B-24, and two Mosquito units, namely the 653rd and the 654th, using PR XVIs delivered in February.

Many of the personnel who were transferred into the 802nd had to be retrained. Mechanics who had never seen a Mosquito night bomber, attended a two-week course at the Rolls-Royce engine school in Derby. Others attended the airframe school at the de Havilland factory in Hatfield. Most of the pilots had flown P-38 Lightning with the 50th FS in Iceland, and were therefore used to the Lockheed figher's contra-rotating propellers. They had never experienced the take-off and landing characteristics of the Mosquito – high landing speed and tendency to swing on take-off. They also had to remember to open the radiator shutters just prior to take-off so as to prevent the engines overheating.

PR XVIs used a two-stage, two speed supercharger that would cut in automatically at altitude. The superchargers were independent on each engine, and a small difference in adjustment caused one to change gears hundreds of feet before the other. The resulting 'bang' and surge of power to one engine could wrest control from the unwary pilot, and give the impression that the aircraft had been hit by flak. Several Airspeed Oxfords and three Mosquito T IIIs were assigned for training.

On 9 August 1944 the 802nd was re-activated as the 25th BG, which, together with the 7th PRG, became part of the 325th PRW, commanded by Col Elliot Roosevelt. The Mosquitoes in the 25th BG operated from Watton almost until war's end – during the last 50 days of European

MM384 lost its port undercarriage during landing at Watton on 4 May 1944, being repaired on site, before being sent to Burtonwood on 8 July 1944 (*via George Sesler*)

'Just dropped in old boy!' PR XVI NS553 suffered a starboard undercarriage failure after putting down in an emergency during the summer of 1943 at the 96th BG base at Snetterton Heath, in Norfolk (*via Dick Jeeves*)

conflict, the unit had also operated from Harrington, in Northamptonshire.

The 653rd Light, Reconnaissance, or 'Light Weather', Sqn flew 1531 varied missions between 28 March 1944 and April 1945, including 1332 flights known as *Blue Stocking*, which were associated with weather observation and forecasting. The balance of its missions comprised command flights, target scouting missions and Chaff dispensing sorties. Chaff was the American equivalent of 'Window', and was dropped over a wide area to 'snow' German fighter control radar and radar-equipped AA guns by using an electric dispensing mechanism in the Mosquito's bomb-bays. Chaff was dispensed over the defence perimeter of a target just before the oncoming bombers arrived. Turning and climbing over the bombers, the PR XVIs then photographed the bomb drop itself in motion picture. They then followed the bombers, taking still photographs of bombardment effectiveness.

The 654th, or the 'Special' squadron, flew 700 varied missions, including 161 night photography flights code-named *Joker* using B-25s, B-26s and PR XVIs. The Mosquito was much more versatile than the two medium bomber types, and was employed on medium and high altitude night photography missions at an average speed of 270 mph. Each PR XVI would carry 12 60-lb Type M-46 photo-flash bombs of 700,000 candlepower in its bomb bay. These were dropped, normally from

Lt Walter D Gernand (right), 654th BS, and his his camerman, Sgt Ebbet C Lynch, 8th CCU, were the first casualties in the 25th BG. They were killed returning from a mission over the D-Day beaches on 6 June 1944 when RS555 hit a railway embankment near High Wycombe (*via George Sesler*)

around 12,000 ft, at eight-second intervals to obtain a 60 per cent running overlap. They were fused to burst at 4000 ft so as to illuminate the target below.

Beginning in early 1943, the RAF had first attempted night photography missions with PR IVs, initially using magnesium flares. Flt Lt John R Myles DFC, AM, RCAF, who was a PR pilot in No 541 (Spitfire) Sqn, and No 544 Sqn, flew a total of 70 operational PR sorties. He confirms;

'All PR flights were made during daylight and were restricted to times between First photographic light and Last photographic light – these

PR XVI NS519/P of the 653rd BS was used by Lt Earl L Muchway and Lt Lionel Proulx – one of two Mosquito crews that accompanied the B-17s on the disastrous *Frantic Joe* shuttle mission to the USSR, Italy and then back to England between 21 June and 5 July 1944. After take-off from San Severo on 5 July, NS519 was forced to abort at 25,000 ft when the port propeller ran away. The aircraft was repaired by an RAF unit and the crew returned to Watton a few days later (*via George Sesler*)

Lt Col Leon W Gray, CO of the 25th BG (23 September 1944 to 14 April 1945) (left), Maj Albert S Straff, Ground Executive, Lt Gen James E Doolittle, Maj Alvin E Podwojski, CO 652nd BS (later Lt Col and deputy Group C), and Col Elliott Roosevelt, wing CO, at Watton (*via G Sesler*)

Lt Elbert F Harris (navigator) and Lt Ron M Nichols (pilot) were the weather scout crew on the second *Frantic* shuttle mission, flown in August. They were shot down by a P-51D Mustang of the 357th FG while returning over France on 8 August, Harris baling out, and with the help of the French Resistance, return on 6 September. Nichols was killed in the encounter (*via George Sesler*)

times varied with the seasons according to sunrise and sunset. Since these times were sometimes restrictive, it was decided to experiment with night photography using magnesium flares, released through a tube in the cockpit floor. The flares were very unstable, and everyone was sceptical about the success of the experiment.'

By 8 September 1943, 29 sorties had been flown for the loss of two aircraft – one of these, DZ600, had been shot down by a Mosquito night-fighter at Ipsden, near Benson, on 28 July, killing both crew. Two PR IXs were then used to perfect the system (once the camera and the flash bombs had been harmonised), using the American flash bombs. These were three times brighter than the British equivalents. Myles continues;

'One night (29 January 1944) my flight commander, Sqn Ldr Bill Aston DFC (who was flying his 175th operational sortie) and Flt Lt Peter Fielding, took off for Germany loaded with six flash bombs and they didn't return. Later, we heard that Aston was a PoW. Apparently, the flash bombs exploded in the plane (PR IX LR430) at 35,000 ft, and the crew were thrown into the air. The pilot wore a seat pack chute and was able to pull the ripcord and land safely. The navigator on the other hand, had a clip-on 'chute, which was still in its rack in the cockpit, and he perished.'

The first USAAF *Joker* mission flown by a Mosquito took place on 28 July 1944 when two volunteer airmen, pilot Richard Geary and navigator

PR XVI NS569/N of the 654th BS/25th BG, at Watton with a 652nd (H) BS B-17 behind (*Flight*)

On 12 August 1944 NS569/N, flown by Lt Robert A Tunnel, 654th BS (left), with photographer Lt David J McCarthy (right), was sent upwards a few hundred feet when the PB4Y-1 *Anvil* mission drone flown by Lt Joseph P Kennedy Jr and 'Bud' Willy, exploded, putting out the Mosquito's port engine and peppering the aircraft with flying debris. McCarthy managed to lower the wheels and Tunnel landed at Halesworth just before the starboard engine cut

Bill Miskho, overflew Lille. They returned safely after two-and-a-half hours, their mission being deemed a complete success. Extensive high altitude photographic missions deep into enemy territory were carried out at around 22,000 ft with the M-46 Flash Bombs fuzed to burst at 6000 ft. Two Type K-19B cameras were installed at a 27° split vertical angle directly over the port holes in the front section of the forward bomb bay. A third K-19B camera was mounted in the rear of the aircraft. These cameras were mounted to tilt to port, starboard and aft.

In addition, a further 55 conventional daylight still-photography sorties were also flown in order to determine the effectiveness of bombing missions, and to observe selected positions, conditions and events. Finally, 20 daylight motion-picture photography flights were undertaken – daylight photography flights, both still and motion-picture, were code-named PRU. The remaining 132 photography missions comprised Chaff dispensing sorties, command flights, secret OSS operations and *Mickey* radar photo-mapping sorties using modified B-17 H2X, sets for it was clear that better maps were needed that showed the same image as a radar scope. By adopting this method, the 25th BG prepared photographic records of radar bombing approaches to a number of high-priority targets deep inside Germany.

After proper annotation, identification and the exact position of the strategic target had been pin-pointed, these *Mickey* bomb-approach-strips, or target run-ups, were used to brief the key radar-navigator-bombardier of the mission so that he could sight the target through the overcast during the actual raid.

The H2X radar scanner was placed in the modified, bulbous nose of the

On 13 August 1944 1Lt Dean H Sanner and 8th CCU cameraman Staff Sgt Augie Kurjack filmed a GB-4 *Batty* 2600-lb glide bombing mission to Le Havre. The GB-4 had a TV camera installed under the nose, and could be guided onto a target from 15 miles distant after being launched from the external wing racks of a B-17. Sanner, in MM370, followed the launched bombs down, and was knocked out of the sky by the explosion of the second *Batty* as he overflew at low-level. The blast threw Sanner out, but Kurjack was killed. He is seen here on the steps of MM370 in happier times (*USAF via George Sesler*)

H2X PR XVI NS538/F with Photo Lab personnel Carl J Wanka and John W Ripley. *Mickey ships* were fitted with modified B-17 H2X sets for preparing photographic records of radar bombing approaches to high-priority targets deep inside Germany. The H2X radar scanner was placed in a bulbous nose, the amplifiers and related equipment in the nose and bomb-bay, and the radar scope in the rear fuselage. There was a tendency for the *Mickey* set to arc or even explode when first turned on. The radar drew a heavier current than the Mosquito's electrical system (*via George Sesler*)

PR XVI NS569/U of the 654th BS crashed on 4 April 1945 (*via Ken Godfrey*)

PR XVI NS619/U of the 25th BG was written off on 23 March 1945 (*via Ken Godfrey*)

Mosquito, the amplifiers and related equipment split between the nose and the bomb-bay, and the radar scope in the rear fuselage. Before the mission, the observer climbed in through the rear door with a camera (sometimes of the motion-picture variety) to photograph the details on the radar screen. The observer's only means of escape in an emergency was to crawl over the set and jump through the bomb-bay – provided the pilot opened the bomb doors! There was a tendency for the *Mickey* set to arc or even explode when first turned on, for the radar drew a heavier current than the Mosquito's electrical system could handle, and aircraft were grounded several times in an attempt to overcome the problem.

Much of the effort by the 654th Sqn was directed towards improving the strategic value of H2X bombing in order to alleviate civilian casualties. *Mickey* had the highest loss rate, highest abort rate and greatest number of failures of any mission involving USAAF PR XVIs – three H2X missions flown at night simply did not return, but there were no losses suffered after December 1944, when *Mickey* switched to daylight operations only, accompanied by a fighter escort (the radar set continued to malfunction, however). Of 36 sorties flown in January, only four were successful, and beginning on 19 February 1945, the 654th switched to light weather missions.

On 24 March 1944, a daylight mission was tried. A Mosquito piloted by Lt C B Stubblefield, and his navigator/radar operator, 1Lt James B Richmond, flew ahead of the Eighth AF bombers, escorted by eight P-51Bs. The Mustangs would be led to the German fighters as they started their climb to attack the bombers, however, leaving the Mosquito to be shot down by a Ninth AF P-47! Stubblefield was killed and Richmond was made a PoW. Later, four P-38 Lightnings were assigned to escort the H2X mission, going in at high altitude.

Meanwhile, in May 1944 the Light Weather Squadron had begun *Blue Stocking* weather operations,

Lt Robert Walker (left) and his navigator, Lt Roy C Conyers (right), of the 654th BS are seen at Watton upon their return from a mission on D-Day +14, along with *Stars & Stripes* and *Yank* magazine combat artist Sgt Scott, who rode home in the nose of the Mosquito after the crew, low on fuel, put down at an airstrip near the Normandy beach head. NS559/M was refuelled by hand using jerry cans earmarked for Gen Patton's tanks (*Pat Walker via Ken Godfrey*)

and immediately prior to D-Day had given weather predictions for the invasion. The Special Squadron also aided in the search for V1 sites in northern France later that summer, performing *Dilly* daylight reconnaissance missions over the Pas de Calais in search of *No-ball* sites. The 654th flew both day and night *Joker* photo and scouting sorties just ahead of the the main bombing force, transmitting up to the minute weather reports back to the task force commander to prevent him leading his bombers into heavy weather fronts. The D-Day invasion was prepared by intelligence gathered on *Dilly* (night photography) missions of coastal defences.

Having carried out one of these missions over the beachhead, Capt Walter D Gernand, a 654th Sqn pilot, and his cameraman, Sgt Ebbet C Lynch, 8th CCU, were killed when RS555 hit a railway embankment near High Wycombe on their return.

H2S installation on board a PR XVI of the 25th BG (*George Sesler*)

The US PR XVIs were also used on daylight missions code-named 'PRU', again using still and motion-picture equipment, and on long-range navigation missions using LORAN (LOng RANge navigation). When, in the summer of 1944, the US Navy needed data on the range, reception and accuracy of the LORAN overlay, 653rd BS PR XVIs fitted with the device accompanied two Eighth AF *Frantic* shuttle bombing missions to the Ukraine on 21 June and 6 August. On the second shuttle mission, Lt Ron M Nichols and Lt Elbert F Harris flew 'scout' for the B-17s. The first leg of the shuttle was made without incident, and the Mosquito crew received good reception on the LORAN from Britain until they reduced height to 6000 ft over Kiev. The Italian chain signal was good at first, then became intermittent until they lost it over Poland.

Air- and groundcrews in the 654th BS/25th BG pose for the camera with 60-lb Type M-46 photo flash bombs of 700,000 candlepower. The PR XVI could carry six of these in the forward half of the bomb-bay, and six in the rear half (*via Ken Godfrey*)

On 18 September 1944 1Lt Robert A Tunnel (pictured) of the 654th BS, with 19-year-old Staff Sgt John 'Buddie' G Cunney, 8th CCU cameraman, failed to return from a PR mission to the Nijmegen-Eindhoven area, where a supply drop was to be made by Liberators to the US Airborne. Tunnel was blinded by a searchlight, lost control and crashed on Plantlunne airfield. Both he and Cunney were killed, and they are interred in the American war cemetery at Neuville en Condroz, Belgium (*via George Sesler*)

While in Russia, Nicholls and Harris flew 'scout' for the B-17s on a bombing mission against a synthetic oil refinery in Poland, then, on 8 August, the shuttle force took off for San Severo, in Italy, on the next leg of the shuttle. Four days later the force flew back to Britain on the last stage of their shuttle, bombing targets in France en route. Nicholls and Harris flew ahead, 'scouting' the weather and reporting back to the bomber leader, but just north of the target area, their PR XVI was shot down by P-51s of the 357th FG, who mistook the Mosquito for a Ju 88. Nicholls was killed when the Mosquito exploded, but Harris survived, and later returned to England with the help of the French Resistance.

Late in September 1944, LORAN Station A in Scotland and Station B in southern England became operational, and the European Synchronised Chain entered service. *Skywave* calibration flights were flown over the continent, which usually saw the Mosquito fly non-stop to San Severo, before returning the next day after refuelling. Maj John Larkin and Lt Claude Moore of the 654th FS flew the first mission to prove the feasibility of reading lines of position (LOP) in the air on 28 September 1944. The missions proved LORAN's capabilities where all other navigational aids had failed. Complete coverage of the continent at all altitudes and in all types of weather was now available to main bomber force.

Both the 653rd and 654th BSs were also used to support the USAAF *Aphrodite* and US Navy *Anvil* pilotless drone operations, which used war-weary B-17s and PB4Y-1s, respectively, packed with 18,000 lb of Torpex – a nitroglycerine compound explosive. The drones were flown to a point over the English coast, or North Sea, where the pilots baled out, leaving the aircraft to fly on towards its target (usually a German weapons site) through the remote control direction of a Ventura 'mother-ship'. Strike analysis depended upon these films to determine the success, or failure, of the mission.

Each of these flights was preceded by a *Blue Stocking* weather reconnaissance sortie over the target by a 653rd BS PR XVI. After the drone was airborne, a Mosquito from the 654th BS would join the mission, carrying an 8th Combat Camera Unit photographer, and they would fly close to

654th Sqn Photo Lab personnel show off their aerial cameras, which they operated from onboard Mosquitoes at Watton. Camera equipment used consisted of the Fairchild K series in the 6-, 12- and 24-in models. Also used was the British F camera with its 36-in lens. For BDA, the Fairchild K20 and K21 hand-held cameras were carried. The radar or *Mickey* camera which provided a photo log of radar imaging, used by the 654th BS, was a development of the Camera Repair Dept at Watton. via Ken Godfrey

the drone to photograph its flight and its point of impact. These images would subsequently be used to improve mission techniques.

The first *Aphrodite* mission, flown on 4 August 1944 against *No-ball* sites, was a disaster. One of the B-17 drones crashed in England, killing its pilot, the second refused to dive over the target and was destroyed by flak, the third overshot and the fourth undershot. Two days later, two more *Aphrodite* drones crashed and exploded, whilst on 12 August, the US Navy's first *Anvil* mission went ahead using a PB4Y packed with 21,170 lb of Torpex and six demolition charges, each containing 113 lb of TNT. Lt Joseph P Kennedy Jr, the eldest son of the former US Ambassador to Britain, and the veteran of a tour with VB-110, and 'Bud' Willy, flew as pilot and co-pilot respectively.

Their target was a secret weapon site at Mimoyecques, which concealed a three-barrelled 150 mm artillery piece designed to fire 600 tons of explosive a day on London. PR XVI NS569, crewed by Lt Robert A Tunnel and Lt David J McCarthy, followed behind the formation of two Ventura 'mother-ships', the PB4Y, a navigational B-17, a P-51 Mustang and a P-38 Lightning. The PB4Y never reached the coast, however, for it inexplicably exploded over Blytheborough at 1500 ft, killing Kennedy and Willy instantly, and scattering debris in the path of the Mosquito, which rose a few hundred feet in the blast. McCarthy was injured but Tunnel was unhurt, and he managed to lower the wheels and land the Mosquito at Halesworth, which was the nearest available airfield.

The next day 1Lt Dean H Sanner and Staff Sgt Augie Kurjack flew to Fersfield in MM370 to film a *Batty* glide-bombing mission to Le Havre. *Batty* was the codename for the 2600-lb GB-4 bomb, which was launched from the wing racks of B-17s, and was fitted with a TV camera under the nose so that it could be guided onto a target from 15 miles away.

When the first bomb was released, Sanner followed it down until it neared the ground. He had to break off when the bomb became erratic, however, and he climbed back to follow the second glide-bomb in. This also proved difficult to follow, and he had trouble keeping the faster

Bad weather during the *Market-Garden* operation made regular air reconnaissance impossible, so 654th BS PR XVIs were instructed to fly over the Arnhem bridge 'every hour on the hour'. On 22 September Lt Pat 'Paddy' Walker (pictured) and Lt Roy C Conyers flew over the northern end at under 500 ft to try to discover who had control of the bridge. Their Mosquito was hit by return fire, but Walker managed to make it back to England and he landed safely at RAF Tangmere (*via Ken Godfrey*)

Mosquito behind the slower glide-bomb, which fell in a marsh and exploded. Sanner's Mosquito was directly overhead at the time, and the force of the blast threw him out of the Mosquito. He suffered a broken leg and injuries to his right arm, and was captured within the hour, finishing the war in *Stalag Luft I*. Sgt Kurjack was killed in the explosion.

In September 1944 the Allies attempted to capture bridges on the Rhine in Holland at Veghel, Grave, Nijmegen and Arnhem, using the 1st British and American 82nd and 101st Airborne Divisions. Operation *Market-Garden* was planned to cut off the Germany Army in the Belgian sector, thus saving the bridges and the port of Antwerp for the American army units and British 30th Corps, which was advancing north from the Dutch border. Bad weather during the *Market-Garden* operation made regular air reconnaissance over the Arnhem bridge impossible, however, so 25th BG Mosquitoes were despatched.

On the morning of 17 September three Mosquitoes took off from Watton – one at 0200, one at 0400 and one at 0600 am – to cover the Nijmegen-Arnhem area. They were tasked with finding the base of the clouds in the area, their thickness, and how low – they were to 'go down to the deck' if necessary, and radio back the information. Next day, when the Germans counter-attacked and forestalled an American attempt to capture the bridge at Nijmegen, five Mosquito weather 'scouts' were despatched to Holland. That night, 1Lt Robert Tunnel and his navigator-cameraman, Staff Sgt John G Cunney, were killed when the pilot was blinded by a 60 cm searchlight over Planlunne airfield, causing him to lose conrol and crash.

On 22 September three Mosquito low-level sorties were ordered to Arnhem bridge to determine, by visual means, whether the German defenders, or British paratroops, controlled the (continued on page 60)

Night Joker photo of Nippes and Essen, Germany, 4/5 October 1944 using M46 photo-flash bombs of 700,000 candlepower, 12 of which could be carried in the bomb bay of a PR XVI. The system was perfected in 1943 by the RAF, using two PR IXs to test the American flash bombs, which were three times brighter than the British equivalents once the cameras and the flash bombs had been harmonised (*Wright Booth via George Sesler*)

COLOUR PLATES

This colour section profiles the photo-reconnaissance units that flew PR Mosquitoes in World War 2. All the artwork has been specially commissioned for this volume, and profile artist Chris Davey and figure artist Mike Chappell have gone to great pains to illustrate the aircraft, and their pilots, as accurately as possible following exhaustive research by the author.

None of the PR Mosquitoes depicted on the following pages have been illustrated in colour artwork before, and the schemes shown have been fully authenticated either by the pilot(s) who flew the aircraft in the frontline, or from contemporary images taken by RAF, RAAF and USAAF photographers, or personnel serving during the period in question.

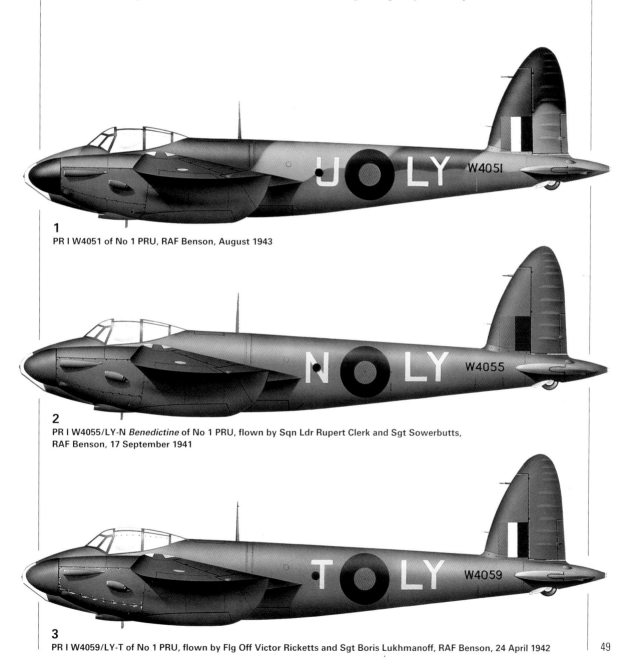

1
PR I W4051 of No 1 PRU, RAF Benson, August 1943

2
PR I W4055/LY-N *Benedictine* of No 1 PRU, flown by Sqn Ldr Rupert Clerk and Sgt Sowerbutts, RAF Benson, 17 September 1941

3
PR I W4059/LY-T of No 1 PRU, flown by Flg Off Victor Ricketts and Sgt Boris Lukhmanoff, RAF Benson, 24 April 1942

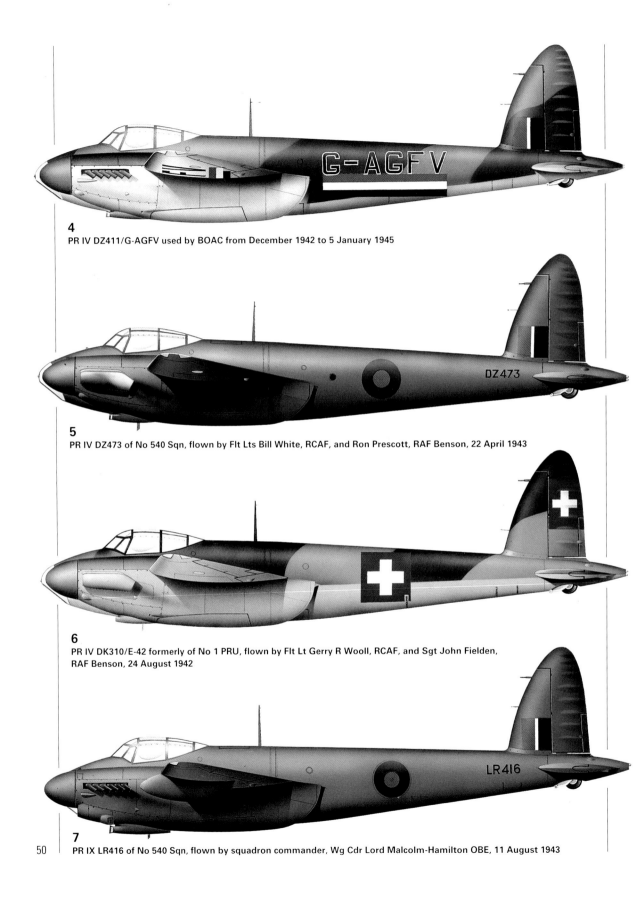

4
PR IV DZ411/G-AGFV used by BOAC from December 1942 to 5 January 1945

5
PR IV DZ473 of No 540 Sqn, flown by Flt Lts Bill White, RCAF, and Ron Prescott, RAF Benson, 22 April 1943

6
PR IV DK310/E-42 formerly of No 1 PRU, flown by Flt Lt Gerry R Wooll, RCAF, and Sgt John Fielden,
RAF Benson, 24 August 1942

7
PR IX LR416 of No 540 Sqn, flown by squadron commander, Wg Cdr Lord Malcolm-Hamilton OBE, 11 August 1943

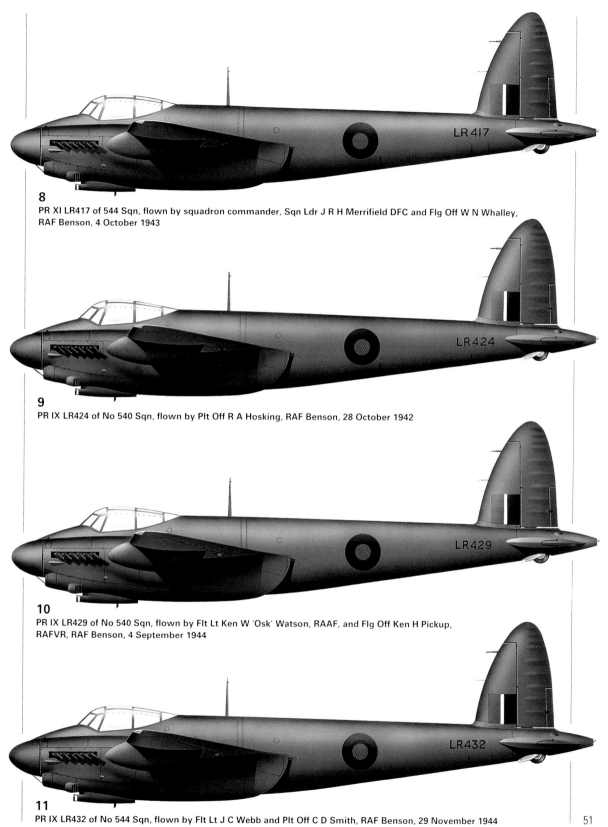

8
PR XI LR417 of 544 Sqn, flown by squadron commander, Sqn Ldr J R H Merrifield DFC and Flg Off W N Whalley,
RAF Benson, 4 October 1943

9
PR IX LR424 of No 540 Sqn, flown by Plt Off R A Hosking, RAF Benson, 28 October 1942

10
PR IX LR429 of No 540 Sqn, flown by Flt Lt Ken W 'Osk' Watson, RAAF, and Flg Off Ken H Pickup,
RAFVR, RAF Benson, 4 September 1944

11
PR IX LR432 of No 544 Sqn, flown by Flt Lt J C Webb and Plt Off C D Smith, RAF Benson, 29 November 1944

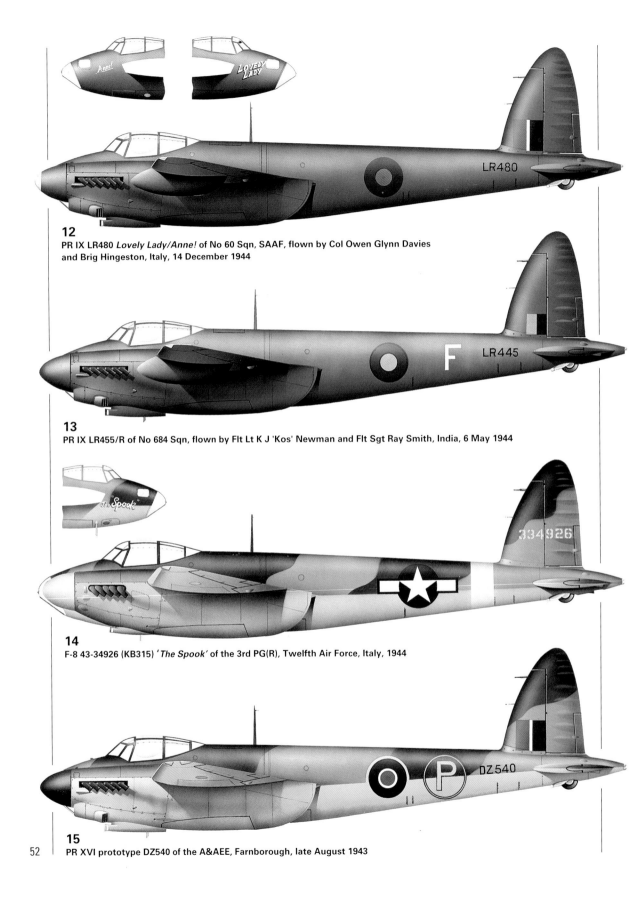

12
PR IX LR480 *Lovely Lady/Anne!* of No 60 Sqn, SAAF, flown by Col Owen Glynn Davies
and Brig Hingeston, Italy, 14 December 1944

13
PR IX LR455/R of No 684 Sqn, flown by Flt Lt K J 'Kos' Newman and Flt Sgt Ray Smith, India, 6 May 1944

14
F-8 43-34926 (KB315) *'The Spook'* of the 3rd PG(R), Twelfth Air Force, Italy, 1944

15
PR XVI prototype DZ540 of the A&AEE, Farnborough, late August 1943

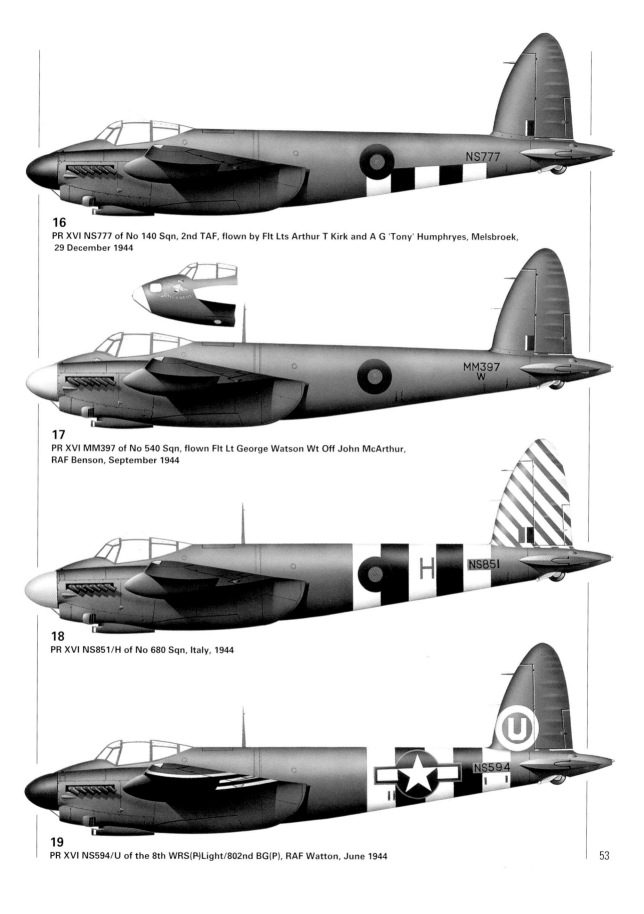

16
PR XVI NS777 of No 140 Sqn, 2nd TAF, flown by Flt Lts Arthur T Kirk and A G 'Tony' Humphryes, Melsbroek,
29 December 1944

17
PR XVI MM397 of No 540 Sqn, flown Flt Lt George Watson Wt Off John McArthur,
RAF Benson, September 1944

18
PR XVI NS851/H of No 680 Sqn, Italy, 1944

19
PR XVI NS594/U of the 8th WRS(P) Light/802nd BG(P), RAF Watton, June 1944

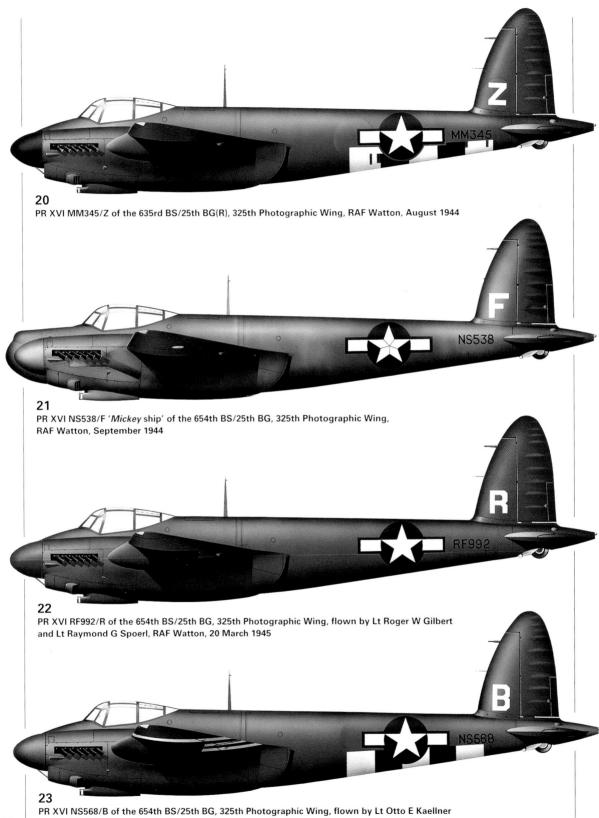

20
PR XVI MM345/Z of the 635rd BS/25th BG(R), 325th Photographic Wing, RAF Watton, August 1944

21
PR XVI NS538/F 'Mickey ship' of the 654th BS/25th BG, 325th Photographic Wing,
RAF Watton, September 1944

22
PR XVI RF992/R of the 654th BS/25th BG, 325th Photographic Wing, flown by Lt Roger W Gilbert
and Lt Raymond G Spoerl, RAF Watton, 20 March 1945

23
PR XVI NS568/B of the 654th BS/25th BG, 325th Photographic Wing, flown by Lt Otto E Kaellner
and Lt Edwin R Cerrutti, RAF Watton, 6/7 November 1944

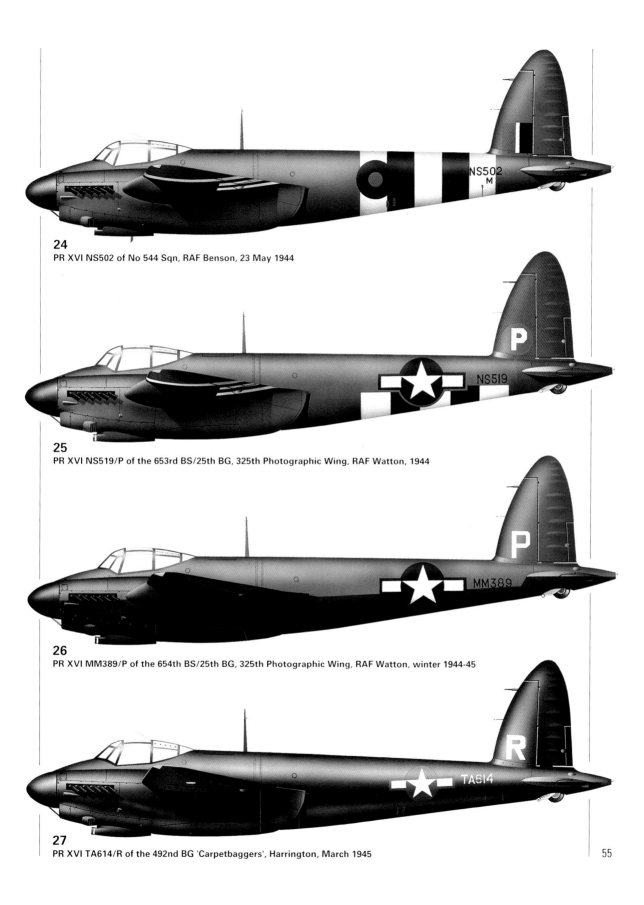

24
PR XVI NS502 of No 544 Sqn, RAF Benson, 23 May 1944

25
PR XVI NS519/P of the 653rd BS/25th BG, 325th Photographic Wing, RAF Watton, 1944

26
PR XVI MM389/P of the 654th BS/25th BG, 325th Photographic Wing, RAF Watton, winter 1944-45

27
PR XVI TA614/R of the 492nd BG 'Carpetbaggers', Harrington, March 1945

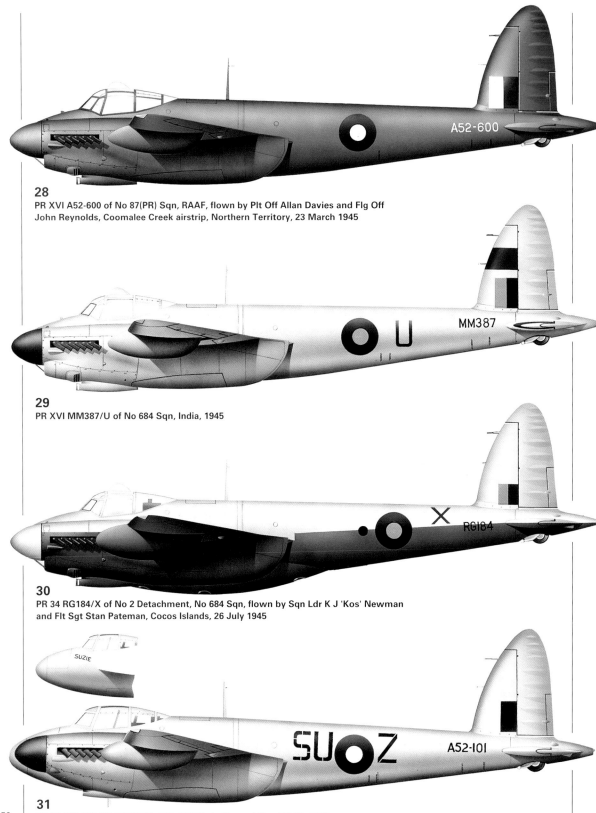

28
PR XVI A52-600 of No 87(PR) Sqn, RAAF, flown by Plt Off Allan Davies and Flg Off
John Reynolds, Coomalee Creek airstrip, Northern Territory, 23 March 1945

29
PR XVI MM387/U of No 684 Sqn, India, 1945

30
PR 34 RG184/X of No 2 Detachment, No 684 Sqn, flown by Sqn Ldr K J 'Kos' Newman
and Flt Sgt Stan Pateman, Cocos Islands, 26 July 1945

31
FB 40 A52-101 SU-Z/*SUZIE* of No 87 (Photo Survey) Sqn, RAAF, 1946

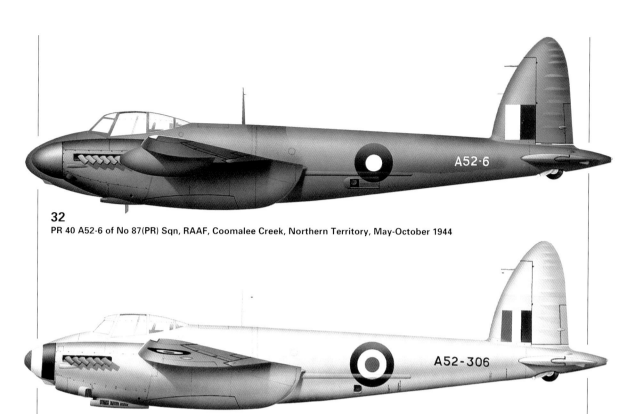

32
PR 40 A52-6 of No 87(PR) Sqn, RAAF, Coomalee Creek, Northern Territory, May-October 1944

33
PR 41 A52-306 of No 87(Photo Survey) Sqn, RAAF, Fairbairn, Canberra, 1950

1
Flt Sgt Lawrence 'Kev' Kevan of
No 680 Sqn at Tocra, near Benghazi,
in September 1944

2
Flt Sgt Frank 'Ginger' Baylis of No 544
Sqn's B Flight at RAF Benson in 1945

3
Flt Lt O M 'Danny' Daniels, RCAF, of
No 544 Sqn's B Flight at RAF Benson
in 1945

4
Lt John M Carter of the 654th
BS/25th BG at RAF Watton in 1944

5
Lt John L Swingen of the 652nd
BS/25th BG at RAF Watton in 1944

6
Lt Robert P 'Paddy' Walker of the
654th BS/25th BG at RAF Watton in
1944.

bridge. Lt Pat 'Paddy' Walker and his navigator, Lt Roy C Conyers, flew over the north end of the bridge, just below the fog, at under 500 ft. They were so low that they could quite easily make out Germans running for their AA guns. Ground fire was encountered almost immediately, and hits were scored on the Mosquito. Their left wing drop tank disintegrated, so Walker jettisoned both stores immediately. The starboard engine then caught fire, and the pilot had to shut it down and feather the propeller. When they were finally out of range, Walker climbed into cloud and limped back to England, where he landed at RAF Tangmere.

On 25 September 1944 another *Blue Stocking* mission was launched as evacuation of the surviving paratroops from Arnhem began. 1Lt Clayborne O Vinyard and 1Lt John J O'Mara took off at 0126 hours in fog so thick they could only see 300 yards in front of them. They flew too deep into Germany, reaching the Frankfurt area before turning back. Having descended to 18,000 ft for the return flight, they were quickly pounced on by a nightfighter, who shot them down – both men baled out and were taken prisoner. On 25 March 1945, 1Lt Bernard J Boucher and his navigator, Louis Pessirilo, were killed during a *Blue Stocking* mission over Germany. Five other Mosquitos on weather reconnaissance returned safely, however.

Some 352 Chaff ('Window') dispensing sorties, code-named, *Gray-Pea* (after Col Leon Gray, who assumed command of the 25th BG on 23 September 1944, and Col (later Gen) Budd Peaslee), were carried out by PR XVI Mosquitos of the 653rd and 654th BS using an electric Chaff dispensing mechanism in their bomb-bays. A formation of three (later four) PR XVIs zig-zagged ahead of the bomber stream, dropped Chaff over the target, and then re-crossed it to photograph the strike – the Mosquitoes were still able to land before the bombers were over the Channel. On 20 March 1945, 2Lt Joseph A Polovick and 1Lt Bernard M Blaum were downed by enemy fire on a *Gray-Pea* mission over Germany and captured.

Exactly two weeks later, six *Gray-Pea* Mosquitos were detailed for Chaff-screening for the Eightth AF, five 'scouted' for the Fortresses and seven flew weather-reconnaissance over the continent and seas around Britain. Lt Col Alvin E Podojski, pilot and Group Deputy Commander, and Capt Lionel A Proulx, navigator, were leading a flight of four Mosquitos on a *Gray-Pea* mission over Kiel when they were attacked by

Lt John M Carter, 654th Sqn pilot, and Lt John L Swingen, 652nd Sqn navigator, pictured on 22 March 1944 (*via George Sesler*)

PR XVI MM386 was delivered to the USAAF at Burtonwood on 4 May 1944 and was assigned to the 653rd BS at Watton, where it was coded 'U'. Combat missions were usually signified on the nose, as here, by a cloud with a red lightning flash. Sometimes, a mosquito caricature with a telescope – a modified representation of the official 653rd BS badge – was used (*the late Jack Green via George Sesler*)

A 25th BG Mosquito starts its engine on a dispersal pan at the 466th BG B-24 Liberator base at Attlebridge, Norfolk, prior to a red tail mission with the Eighth AF in 1945. Some 74 Mosquito sorties code-named, *Red Tail* (after the red tails painted to distinguish them from enemy aircraft), were flown from bases in East Anglia carrying the Command Pilot of Eighth AF bombing missions (*via Mike Bailey*)

German fighters. Although their Mosquito received damage, they managed to reach Sweden safely.

25th BG PR XVIs also flew 74 *Red tail* sorties, which saw the PR XVIs carrying the Command Pilot of Eighth AF bombing missions. By accelerating around his formation in a fast Mosquito bomber, the Command Pilot was provided with the best possible observation platform for greater oversight of the mission. He could better monitor the formation, and advise key pilots of defects in the assembly pattern. In addition, he was not vulnerable to enemy fighters as he might be in a lead bomber. However, enemy fighters were sometimes the least of his concern, for despite the aircraft's prominant red tail markings and US stars, the PR XVIs were often mistaken for Me 262s and Me 410s by bomber gunners and fighter escorts alike.

In an effort to try and prevent identification problems, Mosquito crews were sent to both fighter and bomber group bases to display their distinctive aircraft, but the confusion persisted till war's end. For example, on 4 April 1945, a 653rd BS PR XVI piloted by 1Lt T B Smith, and carrying Col Troy Crawford of the 446th BG, was attacked by Me 262s and was shot down by gunners from the group as the Mosquito moved closer to the B-24s for protection. Both crewmen duly parachuted into captivity.

Lt Col Alvin E Podojski, pilot (right), and Capt Lionel A Proulx, navigator, walk to their waiting Mosquito at Watton. This crew were leading a flight of four Mosquitoes on a *Gray-Pea* mission over Kiel on 3 April 1945 when they were attacked by German fighters, and had to land in Sweden
(*Ken Godfrey via George Sesler*)

Three (later increased to five) PR XVIs were also used in a series of top secret spying missions, code-named *Red Stocking*, which were so-named to help disguise the true nature of their mission, and perhaps persuade the German intelligence services that this was a weather mission similar to *Blue Stocking*. Their true intent was to detect and record UHF transmissions from OSS agents. For this purpose, the bomb-bay was fitted with an oxygen system, and modified to accept a top-secret, and very compact, airborne radio receiver connected to a wire recorder, which was used by an operative who sat on a cramped and uncomfortable drop seat behind the collapsible fuel tank. Entry was through a small hatch on the starboard side of the fuselage, just aft of the wing.

The 'Joan-Eleanor' device, as it was called, had been developed by Lt Cdr Steve Simpson, a Texan scientist, and DeWitt R Goddard. Taking its name from a major in the WACs and Goddard's wife, respectively, the device replaced the cumbersome 'S-Phone' system previously carried in a suitcase by agents in France. 'Joan' weighed only 4 lbs, enabling the agent in the field to carry it easily, and use it to beam transmissions on a radio signal so narrow that it was practically immune to detection. As much information could be passed clearly in one 15-20 minute contact as could be relayed in days by conventional radio.

The first successful contact was made by Simpson in a Mosquito on 22 November 1944 when, circling at 30,000 ft, he recorded the first of eight transmissions with agent 'Bobbie' in Holland. All told, the 654th BS flew 32 *Red Stocking* missions for OSS over Germany and Austria, and enemy occupied territory. One of the most daring was flown on 12 March 1945 when a *Red Stocking* PR XVI, flying at 30,000 ft over Berlin, successfully established radio contact with agents who had earlier been dropped from an A-26C Invader. On 15 March the OSS missions moved to the 492nd BG Liberator base at Harrington, Northamptonshire, but the PR XVIs (and A-26s) remained at Watton for a while longer because of problems maintaining the aircraft at the new site. Crews flew from Watton to Harrington for briefing and after each mission usually returned to Watton.

Altogether, the 25th BG flew 3246 missions, with the 653rd BS losing 24 PR XVIs, including 13 on operations, and the 654th 27 PR XVIs, 16 of them operationally. With the end of the war in Europe, the 25th BG was expected to be sent to to the Pacific, but their PR XVIs were returned to the RAF, and in August the group returned to the USA where, on 8 September 1945, it was inactivated at Drew Field, in Florida.

PR XVI *Greex* in the 492nd BG at Harrington in May 1945 for a clandestine *Red Stocking* operation over Germany. On 13 March 1945 covert operations using the Mosquito moved from Watton to Harrington, but overcrowding, maintenance and political in-fighting deteriorated to such an extent that RAF ground personnel had to be brought in to maintain the aircraft, and OSS regained control over all Mosquito operations (*Art Carnot*)

PASSAGE TO INDIA

One of the myriad problems facing South East Asia Command (SEAC) in India in 1943 was how to perform aerial reconnaissance over Burma and Malaya from its bases in Ceylon and India. Only four camera-equipped B-25C Mitchells of No 681 (PR) Sqn, based at Dum Dum, in Calcutta, possessed the range and speed for such missions over the Bay of Bengal and the Rangoon area. No 681 Sqn's aircraft situation was causing great concern, for the two of the serviceable Mitchells had been in use for over 12 months, and there were no aircraft in the command, other than Mosquitoes, with equivalent operational range and high speed.

After experiencing a delay while Air Ministry approval was sought to allow the conversion of the several Mosquitoes into PR aircraft at No 1 CMU, Kanchrapara, two B IIs, and their flight crews, were transferred in August to the twin-engined flight of No 681 Sqn, followed by three newly-arrived B VIs. All five were fitted with vertical camera mountings, but they did not have the four cameras of the 'PRU type', nor did the additional fuel tanks or, in the case of the B IIs, provision for fitting underwing fuel tanks.

On 23 August 1943, Flg Off Dupee DFM reconnoitered the Mandalay Shewbo-yeu-Monywa-Wuntho area, and the following day a second Mosquito sortie was flown when Flt Lt Picknett over Akyab Island. During September No 681 Sqn flew eight PR sorties over vast areas of Burma, and on occasion a Mosquito VI, which had arrived for trials in August, was also employed. One of the aircraft soon fell victim to enemy action, but after a force-landing, was repaired and returned to Calcutta three weeks later.

The feared deterioration of fuselage bonding adhesives did not happen, despite the aircraft being continually exposed to high temperatures and humidity, so approval was given for the delivery of more Mosquitoes to India.

On 29 September 1943, No 684 Sqn was formed at Dum Dum from the twin-engined flights of No 681 Sqn. While it was planned to have an establishment of 20 PR Mosquitoes, the unit was initially equipped

A high-level PR photo of Port Blair, and its airfield, in the Andaman Islands, photographed by Flt Lt F W Guy DFC and Plt Off Gerald Stevens of No 684 Sqn on a sortie from Cox's Bazaar on 27 March 1944 – part of a 1352-mile round trip (*Stevens' Collection*)

On 22 March 1944 Flt Lt Robin Sinclair and Flg Off Reggie W Stocks were briefed to reconnoitre southwards along the Siam-Singapore railway as far as petrol and prudence allowed. This trip, flown in PR XVI NS688/Q (pictured), reached into northern Malaya and established a record for that time of 2490 miles, lasting 8hr 45min. Sinclair and Stocks landed back at advance base with 30 gallons of petrol remaining. This was the first sortie by an RAF aircraft over Malaya since the fall of Singapore

A long-focus camera being mounted into a PR Mosquito of No 684 Sqn by LACs R Perry and E Smith (*Brt Off*)

with four B-25 Mitchell IIIs, two Mosquito IIs and three VIs. Photographic coverage of targets such as Bangkok and Sumatra could only be reached by the Mosquito PR IX, which had a safe range in excess of 1250 miles. Therefore, LR440 (the first PR IX) was delivered to No 684 Sqn on 18 October – a second crashed the same day on landing at Ranchi, killing the crew. Three days later No 684 performed the first of 33 PR sorties over Burma when Flt Lt F B McCulloch and Sgt T S Vigers flew in LR440 over Rangoon and Magwe. A second PR IX (LR463) arrived on 23 October.

On the 24th, McCulloch and Flt Lt Henry Reeves (again in LR440) reconnoitred the Andaman Islands to bring back photos of Japanese shipping and flying boat activity. Three Ki-43 'Oscar' fighters tried to intercept the high flying Mosquito, but none got near the British aircraft. Later that day, Flt Sgt Johnson and Sgt Willis (in Mk II DZ696) returned safely with photos of Rangoon despite another attempted interception by two fighters, and AA fire at 27,000 ft.

No 684 Sqn's first Mosquito loss on operations from India occurred on 2 November 1943 when Mk II DZ697/J, with Flg Offs Fielding and Turton aboard, failed to return from a photo recce of the Rangoon area. Two days later the supply route from Moulmein to the Sittang bridge was covered by PR IX HJ759/W. All Mosquito operations came to an abrupt end on 12 November, however, when a series of accidents resulted in a signal being sent to all units grounding the aircraft, pending inspection.

On 9 December the six remaining Mosquitos, and four B-25Cs, of No 684 Sqn moved to Comilla, in East Bengal, where it formed part of No 171 PR Wing, Air Command SE Asia, which had come into being on 16 November. No 681 Sqn, meanwhile, moved east also to Chandina. No 684 Sqn's stay at Comilla was to be a short one, for after just month it returned to Dum Dum on 30 January 1944. Their time at the new base was marred by the loss of two crews, the first of which was lost on 10 December when the last Mosquito II (DZ696/S), flown by Sgt Boot with Sgt Wilkins, was shot down over Rangoon. The second aircraft (Mosquito, Mk VI HJ760/Y) crashed near Feni on 23 December following structural failure, killing Flg Off Orr and Sgt Johnson.

Operations now covered distances of up to 1000 miles from base, and an eight-hour duration was not uncommon. On 15 December, unit CO, Sqn Ldr Basil S Jones, and Flg Off R C Hawson, used LR463/A to reconnoitre Bangkok for the first time. The sortie revealed new information on Japanese reserve positions, and the use of 'lay-back' airfields, and earned both men the DFC.

In February 1944 the PR Force (PRF) was formed under Gp Capt S G Wise to bring together Nos 681 and 684 Sqns, and the US 9th PRS. No 684, now back at Dum Dum, and commanded by Wg Cdr W B Murray, received nine pressurised PR XVIs, which enabled higher altitudes to be flown. The remaining Mk VIs were retired, and they became a valuable source of spares, as parts were always in short supply. At the beginning of the month No 684 Sqn had begun a photographic survey of Burma, while reconnaissance flights to islands in the Indian Ocean also continued.

Cameras being examined by LACs Harris and D Fisher of No 684 Sqn. (*Brt Off*)

On 7 February Sqn Ldr Basil Jones DFC and Flg Off R C Hawson DFC, in PR IX LR440/V, tussled with a 'Hamp' fighter over Port Blair, in the Andaman Islands. Later that same day, NS497/J was intercepted and the crew forced to abort the mission to the Bangkok area. On 23 February PR IX 'L' returned from a 'Special Areas' sortie with engine trouble and had to be written off. Two days later, Flt Lt F B McCulloch and Flt Sgt T S Vigers, in LR493/P, flew to Mergui, then south down the coastal road to Tavoy, where they were intercepted by five Zeros at 22,000 ft. McCulloch climbed away, and they were not attacked.

Flg Offs Jack Winship RCAF and Peter Haines had been involved at Cawnpore with experiments to attach a 90-gal jettison tank under the belly of a PR IX (MM254). Using this tank on LR443, the crew took off from Dum Dum on 29 February and flew across the Bay of Bengal on a recce of the Andaman Islands, with a stop at Ramu. Duration of the flight was 8hr 25min, and the return flight was flown in the most violent weather Winship had encountered. He and Haines covered Port Blair, Stewart Sound and Port Bonington, before meeting a Zero, which was unable to catch them. Another PR IX, LR463/N, developed engine trouble on the outward flight and later had to be struck off charge. By the end of the month few Mosquitoes were available due to a shortage of spares.

In March 1944 No 684 Sqn made regular flights to the Andaman Islands and reconnoitred the Japanese railway system in Burma. On the 22nd, Flt Lt Robin Sinclair and Flg Off Reggie W Stocks were briefed to reconnoitre southwards along the Siam-Singapore railway as far as petrol and prudence allowed. This trip, flown in PR XVI NS688/Q, reached into northern Malaya and established a record for that time of 2490 miles, lasting 8hr 45minutes. Sinclair and Stocks landed back at advance base with 30 gallons of petrol remaining. This was the first sortie by an RAF aircraft over Malaya since the fall of Singapore.

Robin Sinclair, who was the son of Sir Archibald Sinclair Bart, Secretary of State for Air in Winston Churchill's wartime cabinet, made many social contacts in Calcutta. Indeed, he often brought interesting

Wt Off Davison, a navigator in No 684 Sqn, is seen about to board PR IX MM295/C on the brick paved area of Alipore during a lull in the monsoon rains. On 27 March 1944, Flt Lt 'Kos' Newman RNZAF and Flt Sgt Ron Smith flew a 1860-mile trip in PR XVI MM295/C to photograph a stretch of the Burma railway and airfields at Bangkok and Hua Hin (*via Geoff Thomas*)

people into the mess, including the Maharajahdirajah of Burdwan (whose palace was used as the squadron airmens' mess) and the monocled Colonel Bernard Fergusson, one of the Chindit leaders.

Five days after this epic flight, on 27 March, Flt Lt Kossuth 'Kos' J Newman RNZAF and Flt Sgt Ron Smith in No 684 Sqn flew a 1860-mile trip in PR XVI MM295/C to photograph a stretch of the Burma railway, and airfields at Bangkok and Hua Hin. On the same day, Sqn Ldr J A Johnson and Flt Sgt F Wells, in MM296/M, flew a sortie to

Central Bangkok, photographed from 28,000 ft by Flt Lt F W Guy DFC and Plt Off Gerald Stevens on 24 May 1944, part of a 1720-mile round trip from Chittagong (*Stevens Collection*)

the Nicobars to cover Port Blair airfield and the radar site at Mount Augusta. The final sortie of March (flown on the 31st) saw Flg Offs Dupee DFM and McDonnell, in MM296, obtain the first photos of Car Nicobar Island.

In April No 684 Sqn experimented with long-range flights as far afield as Khun Khaen, in central Siam, and Vientiane, in Laos, to see if they could fly over the monsoon weather so as to cover Japanese rear areas when the weather had passed. Until 13 April these sorties were flown from Dum Dum, but then Ramu in the south was used. The Mosquitoes flew in the evening before their sorties so that they could take-off at first light and reach their objectives early in the day before cloud built up.

On 4 April Sgt T Cocks and Flt Sgt G Smith, in NS497/J, set out to cover Mergui, but found the Tenasserim coast covered in cloud. On the return journey, however, they photographed the Mokpalin area and the Sittang bridge on the Burma railway, which had been damaged during a recent bombing raid. Their photos revealed that repairs had been carried out and the rail line was free between Martaban and Rangoon. Four days later the bridge was heavily bombed by B-24s. A PR carried out on 10 April by Wt Off J A Johnson and Flt Sgt F Wells, in LR445/F, showed that the two western spans of the bridge had been destroyed. (the same day MM296 crashed on take-off from Dum Dum).

Meanwhile, on 5 April, Flg Offs Jack Winship and Peter Haines, now on their second op, in MM294/H, had a close call during a sortie from Dum Dum, via Ramu, to cover Kaun Gean and some new enemy airfields in north-east Siam. Winship explains;

In August 1944, because the weather over the Indian Ocean was clearer than over the Bay of Bengal, a detachment was sent to operate from China Bay, Ceylon, for operations in No 222 Group. The detachment's task was to make the first air survey of northern Sumatra, and nearby islands. The Ceylon detachment began operations on 15 August when PR IX LR467/R flew a recce of Nancowry and Sabang Islands

PR XVI RG137 taxying out
(*via Geoff Thomas*)

'We picked up a very strong tail wind on the way out and, after two hours flying, had travelled 780 miles, at which point we lost our port engine. This prevented us from transferring the fuel in our 50-gal drop tanks to our main tank, and we had to jettison 100 gallons of very precious fuel. Things were pretty shaky for the first hour or so of our

Sabang, northern Sumatra, photographed from 28,000 ft on 10 October 1944 by Flt Lt F W Guy DFC and Plt Off Gerald Stevens, part of a 1970-mile round trip from Trincomalee, Ceylon (*Stevens Collection*)

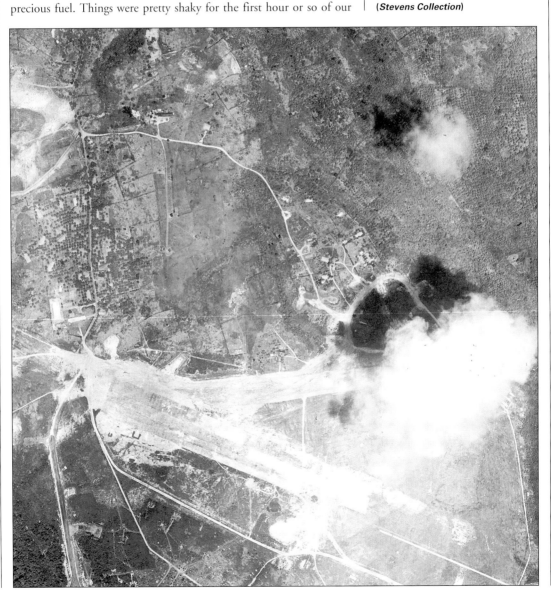

RG176, pictured in January 1945 with 200-gal wing drop tanks during trials at the A&AEE, was the first PR 34 and it flew on 4 December 1944. In May 1950 the aircraft was converted to a PR 34A by Marshalls, before being issued to No 540 Sqn at Benson, who used RG176 from July 1951 to June 1952, when, after an accident, it was reduced to spares by No 58 MU
(*DH via Philip Jarrett*)

780-mile return trip. We did a gradual descent to around 12,000 ft and, after some fine tuning, the good old Mossie settled down and purred along beautifully. We made the trip back to the landing ground at Ramu in a little over four hours.'

This feat earned a commendation from Air Commander EAC, Maj Gen George E Stratemeyer.

In May 1944 a No 684 Sqn detachment began operations from Alipore, a suburb of Calcutta. On the 6th Flt Lt Kos Newman and Flt Sgt Ray Smith, in LR445/R, took off to fly a reconnaissance sweep of Nancowry Harbour, in Great Nicobar, to ascertain as to whether or not there were any Japanese shipping in port. Ray Smith recalls;

'The trip (2256 miles) was thought to be at the extreme range of the PR IX, and at the time it was felt that we might not be able to get back to our advanced landing ground at Ramu from where we had taken off. To cover this contingency, the Royal Navy had placed caches of food and survival kits on some islands off the Arakan coast. If we thought that we would not be able to make it back to Ramu, we were to make a forced landing on the sea adjacent to one of these islands and, hopefully, we would be picked up by the Royal Navy. Fortunately, we were able to make it back, although we flew for about ten minutes with our fuel gauges reading zero.'

This flight earned Newman the DFC and Smith the DFM.

No 684 Sqn received some additional PR XVIs in May and June, which was just as well for on 9 June LR463 was lost in a crash. By this time the monsoon weather was affecting the number of successful operations being flown, and 81 of the 110 sorties in June were abortive. On 6 July MM343/W crashed on take-off. On 22 July Flg Offs Tebb and Fletcher, in MM392/K, fitted with a 90-gal jettison tank, reconnoitered three airfields on the Andaman and Nicobar islands.

At the beginning of August a No 684 Sqn detachment was based at Yelahanka, near Bangalore, in southern Indi,a for aerial survey work. The weather over the Indian Ocean was clearer than over the Bay of Bengal, so, on 11 August, the squadron sent a detachment from Alipore to China Bay, Ceylon, for operations with No 222 Group. The detachment's task was to to make the first air survey of northern Sumatra and nearby islands. To ease maintenance and processing problems, the Yelahanka detachment also moved to China Bay a few days later. The Ceylon detachment

Another photo of the railway, taken on 29 March, from 100 ft, using a forward-facing oblique camera mounted in the nose of the PR XVI (*Stevens Collection*)

A bridge on the central Siam railway, near Uttardit, was destroyed by aerial bombardment, and photographed on 29 March 1945 from 100 ft (*Stevens Collection*)

began operations on 15 August when PR IX LR467/R flew a recce of Nancowry and Sabang Islands. Eight days later the same Mosquito flew to Sabang and Car Nicobar, while on the 25th, PR XVI MM228/D flew to Sabang and along the west coast of Sumatra to Sibolga harbour. A further lengthy sortie to Sumatra the following day discovered a previously unknown Japanese airfield at Padang Tidji, near Sigli.

By the end of August, however, the Mosquitoes had almost ceased operations due to the monsoon. In spite of the weather, on the 28th Sqn Ldr Kos Newman and Flt Sgt Ray Smith, in PR XVI NS622/Y, covered a section of the Burma-Siam railway adjacent to the side of a mountain just south of Moulmein. They came under heavy AA fire and were lucky to escape, as Ray Smith recalls;

'We were greeted with intense anti-aircraft fire whilst flying at about 500 ft, and just as we had completed the job the aircraft was hit in the port engine and also in the nose, smashing Kos's oxygen economiser. Not knowing the extent of the damage which had been caused to the port engine, we climbed to 25,000 ft, since we did not want to get caught at low altitude with only one engine functioning properly. We then decided to try and make our way to Chittagong, above the Irawaddy valley, where we felt that the weather would not be quite so severe. We were right in this assumption, and upon successfully reaching the Chittagong area, we decided to carry on to our base at Alipore, as the port engine appeared to be functioning normally. Whilst we were flying at high level, we both had to use my oxygen supply alternately as became necessary.'

As a result of this remarkable mission, the area was heavily bombed a few days later, which caused a land slide that completely blocked the track. Newman was awarded a bar to his DFC.

No 684 Sqn's activities at China Bay were halted until mid-September 1944, when a PR of parts of Sumatra was flown, and were then halted again until October. That month, No 684 Sqn Mosquitos at Alipore used Cox's Bazaar, at the mouths of the Ganges, to make long-range flights into Burma. Flt Lt Terence Boughton, and his

navigator, Sgt W F 'Bill' Rhodes, who had joined No 684 Sqn in July, flew their first op on 6 September – a survey of the Japanese-held Mandalay area. Boughton recalls;

'Flying up and down parallel lines at a mere 10,000 ft or so was a bit anxious, but no one seemed interested in us, and we did a second trip over the Chindwin River a few days later. By October we were venturing further afield, moving forward to Cox's Bazaar to fill up with fuel, and then usually spending the night in grass-roofed huts, before taking off early in the morning. From here we could cover Rangoon, Moulmein, Akyab, Chiengmai and as far south as Bangkok.

The Mudon pagoda, pictured by Wg Cdr Lowry and Plt Off Stevens on 1 June 1945 (*Gerald Stevens Collection*)

This was very high-altitude work using long-focus cameras to photograph ports, railways, roads and airfields. – on one occasion, however, we had to cover the road from Chiengmai to Hluang, in northern Thailand, from just 5000 ft. Our extreme range took us down to Victoria Point and Phuket. We flew photographic sorties as far as Bangkok and northern Thailand. About this time the wooden glued-together Mosquitoes were giving trouble, and there were cases of wings collapsing. So I was sent to Columbo on a ship recognition course.'

In November 1944 Wg Cdr Lowry assumed command of No 684 Sqn. All Mosquito operations came to an abrupt halt on 12 November, however, when yet another signal to all units required Mosquito aircraft to be grounded, pending inspection. The cause of the accidents was supposedly destruction by 'termites' and deterioration of glue, but the actual cause resulted from faulty construction of the wing spar. The number of aircraft available to No 684 Sqn, for instance, dropped from 21 in October to just four airworthy PR IXs by 20 November.

With the arrival of refurbished and replacement aircraft, the squadron soon had 12 Mosquitoes available for operations again, and in January 1945 No 684 Sqn flew over 70 sorties, including 2100-mile round trips to survey Phuket Island, which had been first covered on 30 December.

The Thanbuziat to Banpong part of the Burma-Siam railway through 244 miles of jungle, photographed by a PR Mosquito (*Denis Coram Collection*)

Sqn Ldr Newman and Flt Sgt Williams, in NS622/X, obtained complete coverage of Phuket on 5 January during a round trip of 2286 miles. No 1 Detachment at China Bay, near Trincomalee in Ceylon, made similar long-range sorties to the Andaman and Nicobar islands and the tip of Sumatra, flying almost 1000 statute miles across the Bay of Bengal – each sortie lasted more than eight hours. Flt Lt

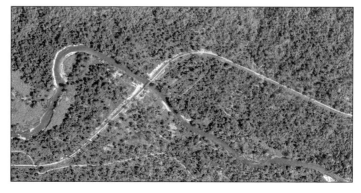

At the beginning of June 1945 the PR Development Flight was formed at Ratmalana in Ceylon with two PR XVIs and two Oxfords, under the command of Flt Lt Henry Lowcock (centre) (*Denis Coram Collection*)

Terence Boughton, who was posted to China Bay on 13 February, recalls;

'Our aircraft were fitted with drop tanks from Hurricanes under the fuselage – rather bluff and draggy things, which got us on a couple of hundred miles and were then dropped into the ocean (during low-level sorties over the Burma- Siam railway in February, the tanks were also used for carrying a forward-facing F24 oblique camera). We were then back on internal fuel, plus the well streamlined underwing drop tanks, which we didn't drop as there weren't any more available.

'For these trips we were kitted out with jungle survival suits, revolvers, booklets and cards in various Far Eastern languages, and bags of Maria Theresa silver dollars, which were apparently acceptable everywhere. If we had had trouble 1000 miles from home, we should probably have done well to land on a beach and survive as best we could, for the Bay of Bengal was utterly empty of shipping, although there was a slim chance of being picked up by one of the Dutch Catalina flying boats from the squadron which was also based at China Bay. These were slow, but had an immense endurance and flew regularly across to Sumatra which, before the Japanese invasion, was part of the Dutch overseas empire.'

On 10 February the detachment commander, Flt Lt Henry C Lowcock, and his navigator, Flt Sgt D W R Lewin, photographed five Sumatran airfields. Four days later Wg Cdr Lowry DFC and Flt Lt Gerald Stevens flew the first of a series of low-level reconnaissance flights over the notorious Burma-Siam railway. By the end of February, No 684 Sqn was back to full strength with 22 Mosquitoes, including three which were detached to China Bay. By March 1945 record-breaking flights of around nine hours were made to Phuket Island to reconnoitre possible landing beaches.

The approaching monsoon, and

Three PR 34s left the UK for India on 29 May 1945, and after their flight in RG185/Z was delayed 24 hours by engine problems, Sqn Ldr Kos Newman DFC* and Wt Off Ray Smith flew the fourth PR 34, and established a new England-India record of 12 hr 25 min. Pictured in India at the end of the record-flight are the four crews: left to right, Flt Lt Danny Daniels, his navigator, Wt Off Frank Baylis (who flew RG186), Wt Off Reg Smith, Flt Lt A Weatherill, Sqn Ldr Kos Newman DFC*, Flg Off Les Grover, Flt Lt Neville Polley and Flg Off A G Shingles (*Baylis Collection*)

build up of tropical storms in the Bay of Bengal, caused operational problems. On 10 March Flt Lt Jack Irvine and Flt Sgt Bob Bannister flew through one such storm to photograph possible landing beaches on Phuket Island during a flight that lasted almost nine hours. Twelve days later, Irvine and Bannister carried out a sortie which lasted 8hr 45min, and covered 2493 miles, to photograph the Bangkok-Singapore railway to a point just south of the Malayan border. Terence Boughton adds;

'These trips across the water continued through the spring of 1945. On several we met the intertropical front, a fearsome barrier of cloud which reached from the sea up to above our cruising level, and caused heavy airframe and carburettor icing, forcing us to turn back. On 4 April we had an unusual task – a very low-level sortie with an oblique camera, flying along the coast of Camorta Island at a mere 1000 ft. I have no idea what we were looking for as the island appeared to be utterly deserted.

'In all this work Bill Rhodes handled the navigation, the radio (except for short range VHF) and the photography; flying the aeroplane was comparatively relaxed although we had no autopilot, and there were long hours of holding a steady course and height, and occasionally watching the fuel gauge.'

Next day, 5 April, Flt Lt R Stoneham and Flg Off R Burns, in NS657/A, had a lucky escape. At the beginning of their run along the Burma-Siam railway, their starboard engine speed began to increase from 2000 to 3000 rpm. Stoneham throttled back but this had no effect.

PR 34 RG245 in flight. The PR 34 was the ideal aircraft for long-range operations in the Far East. All armour and fuel tank bullet-proofing was deleted, and 1192 gallons of fuel in tanks in bulged bomb bay and two 200-gal drop tanks under the wings gave a still air range of 3600 miles, cruising at 300 mph (*Author's Collection*)

PR 34 RG203 of No 684 Sqn is towed into position on the Cocos Islands. The first four PR 34s were taken on charge by No 684 Sqn, and on 3 July 1945 RG185/Z, flown by the CO, Wg Cdr W E M Lowry DFC, and Flt Sgt Stan Pateman, made the first sortie from Cocos Island. By the end of July 25 sorties had been carried out, and 13 more by VJ-Day. Sorties were usually in the region of nine hours duration (*via Geoff Thomas*)

PR 34 VL618 in overall PRU Blue in flight, showing the five underbelly circular windows for vertical and oblique cameras. All PR 34s carried four split F 52 vertical cameras – two forward, two aft – of the belly tank, and one F 24 oblique camera (or, alternatively, a vertical K 17 camera for air survey) aft also
(*BAe via Jerry Scutts*)

Wt Off Ray Smith (left) and Sqn Ldr Kos Newman DFC* (right). Operating from the Cocos Islands, on 4 July 1945, they covered the airfields at Kuala Lumpur and Port Swettenham and, on the return flight, Fort de Kock airfield, north of Padang in Sumatra. On 16 July they obtained satisfactory cover of Jahore Bharu and Singapore Island (*Ray Smith Collection via Eddie Leaf*)

Propeller pitch was altered with the same result, and the Mosquito began vibrating as the engine speed reached 5,000 revs. Burns, who was in the nose, saw that the engine was on fire, and the extinguisher was operated. The aircraft lost height rapidly and, by the time it cleared the coast near Moulmein, was down to 1000 ft. A height of 600 ft was maintained over the Gulf of Martaban and, when land was again sighted near Basseir, Stoneham jettisoned the wing-tanks, enabling the aircraft to climb to 1500 ft and return to Cox's Bazaar.

On 18 April 1945 Flt Lt Newman and Flt Sgt Preston in RG125/V were killed on a sortie from Alipore to Cox's Bazaar when their Mosquito crashed in bad weather en route. Four days later Flt Lt T Bell and Flg Off J Plater, in NS675/Z, were lost in similar circumstances on a sortie to Nancowry Island – it was assumed that they had crashed into the sea. That same day, Flt Lt Stoneham and Flg Off Burns, in NS646/I, had another lucky escape when they were caught in severe storms en route to Victoria Point. They returned to Cox's Bazaar with only ten minutes' fuel remaining. The Mosquito's leading wing edges and tailplane were damaged, requiring repairs before the crew could continue to Alipore.

Operation *Dracula* – the seaborne invasion to capture Rangoon – took place on 1/2 May 1945, but No 684 Sqn's PR IXs were grounded throughout this period by a particularly severe tropical storm. Gradually, conditions improved proved, and by the end of the month the Mosquitoes, using Kyaukpyu, on Ramree Island, as an advanced landing strip, were flying regularly as far as Bangkok, Phuket Island and the Siam railway. Most of the sorties were carried out by the China Bay detachment, which continued its coverage of the Indian Ocean islands.

On 24 May Wg Cdr W E M Lowry DFC and his navigator, Flg Off Gerald Stevens, in NS622/X, flew to Tenasserim and Kra, via the advanced landing ground at Kyaukpyu, to take high level v erticals, before dropping to just 50 ft for oblique photos of St Luke, St Matthew and the Domel Islands. On 28 May Flg Off Cliff G Andrews RNZAF and Wt Off H S Painter, in RG125/V, reconnoitered targets in the Siam Valley, and covered Don Muang airfield at Bangkok, the water-front at Sattahib and bridges on the Bangkok-Phnom Penh railway line. A 'first-sighting' message was radioed back about shipping observed at Sattahib. As a result, Liberators made attacks on two merchant ships and the port installations on 30 May and 1 June.

In early June 1945, the PR Development Flight was formed at Ratmalana, in Ceylon, with two PR XVIs and two Oxfords, under the command of Flt Lt Henry Low-

cock. Flt Lt Terrence Boughton, who (with Bill Rhodes) had flown his last trip on 18 May, was one of the pilots assigned to the Flight;

'I had a short spell taking pictures of beaches in Celyon by the so-called transparency method (pioneered by the PRU in Europe and the Mediterranean), which enabled beach gradients to be deduced from wave patterns. This was in preparation for the invasion of western Malaya, called Operation *Zipper* (which was due to take place in September 1945).'

Before the invasion could go ahead, No 684 Sqn had to obtain full coverage of a ten-mile stretch of coastline in the region of Port Swettenham, on the east coast of Malaya. A new Mosquito – the PR 34, a VLR version of the PR XVI – was available, and if based on the Cocos Islands, 1050 miles south-west of Singapore, reconnaissance missions to Kuala Lumpur and Port Swettenham were possible. On 27 March Sqn Ldr Kos Newman and Wt Off Ray Smith returned to England to test the aircraft's suitability. They flew back in PR IX LR464 (which they had brought out in December 1943) so it could be inspected by de Havillands to determine how Mosquitoes were coping with tropical conditions. Wt Off Ray Smith recalls;

'We found the PR 34 to be entirely suitable to our requirements, and at dusk on the evening of 29 May we took off from Benson for Karachi (in RG185/Z) in company with three other aircraft crewed by UK personnel,

PR 34 RG307 which was written off after a heavy landing (*Denis Moore Collection*)

refuelling at Cairo West. This flight was to take the form of a race to establish a new England to India record. After we had been airborne for a short time, however, our starboard engine started giving trouble, and Kos decided that he would have to feather the propeller and return to Benson on one engine. The only problem with that was that we had about three tons of fuel on board, so it was decided to continue until we were over the Channel and jettison the drop tanks. We were over complete cloud cover at the time,

PR 34 RG247 suffered a similar fate (*Denis Moore Collection*)

A52-600 of No 87 Sqn RAAF at
Moratai on 4 August 1945, staging
through to Labuan Island, Borneo,
on detachment from Coomalee
Creek, Northern Territory, to 1st
Tactical Air Force, RAAF. Eleven
operations over Borneo were
completed in ten days, flown in two
Mosquitoes on the detachment,
A52-604 and A52-600
(*Allan L Davies*)

and my ETA for the Channel coast was slightly out, culminating in our dropping the drop tanks on a farm in Kent. From the farmer's point of view, it was a pity that the tanks did not remain intact.

'Kos had never landed a Mosquito at night on two good engines, let alone one. On the final approach to the runway, he asked me to call out the airspeed and altitude for every 50 ft of descent, to enable him to give his undivided concentration to the actual flying. I had just uttered the words, "120 and 50 ft" when we came into violent contact with the end of the runway, but Kos rectified the situation in his own inimitable manner, and we were once again safely back on terra firma, and so to bed. The following day we received information that the fastest time put up by one of the other three aircraft was 12hr 27min. The fault on our starboard engine having been rectified, we took off again that evening and did the trip in 12hr 25min, thus establishing a new England to India record.'

The four PR 34s were taken on charge by No 684 Sqn which, on 9 June 1945, became part of No 347 (PR) Wing, RAF. During June No 684 was able to fly only six sorties from Alipore. On the 16th Flt Lts G Edwards and Jack Irvine flew north to the peak of Makalu, in Nepal, then to Mt Everest, ten miles further west. Edwards circled the mountain for 20 minutes, taking photographs with cameras mounted in wing-tanks. Nepal was a neutral country, and the Everest flights (Wg Cdr D B Pearson of No 681 Sqn had flown over Everest on 26 May in a Spitfire) caused a minor diplomatic upset when details were released to the Press. It was explained that the aircraft were lost, due to the extensive cloud cover, and were only able to fix their positions by recognising the mountain.

On 28 June 1945 the four PR 34s flew from Alipore, via China Bay, to the Cocos Islands, arriving the next day, and forming (No 2) Detachment at the recently-completed airstrip. No 3 Detachment was established at Chittagong in July, but bad weather prevented all except one sortie being flown. On 1 July another flight was made to Mount Everest by two Mosquitoes from Alipore – one aircraft was fitted with cine cameras – but heavy cloud and snowstorms prevented a clear view of the mountain.

On 3 July PR 34 RG185/Z, flown by Wg Cdr W E M Lowry DFC and Flt Sgt Stan Pateman, flew the first reconnaissance sortie from Cocos Island, when they covered Point Pinto, via Morib, and the Port Swettenham area, via Gedong, and finally Sumatra. Next day Kos Newman and Ray Smith covered the airfields at Kuala Lumpur and Port Swettenham and, on the return flight, Fort de Kock airfield, north of Padang , in Sumatra. Ray Smith recalls;

'The trips from the Cocos Islands were usually in the region of nine hours' duration. We used to make for Suncling Island, off the coast of Sumatra, 613 miles from Cocos, and then set course to the particular area we were required to cover, the idea being that if an aircraft had to ditch, the ASR Catalina, based in the Cocos and crewed by a Dutch crew, would know along which track to search for survivors.'

On 10 July 1945 a fifth PR 34 (RG191/M) joined the No 2 Detachment on the Cocos Islands, but on the 14th, flying out on a sortie, the port engine began vibrating when 450 miles from base. The pilot, Flt Lt Edwards, feathered the propeller and jettisoned his wing-tanks, but the aircraft lost height and crashed in the sea on final approach. For several days the Mosquitoes' objectives over areas of western Malaya, in preparation for Operation *Zipper*, were cloud-covered, but Sqn Ldr Newman and Wt Off Reg Smith, in RG185/Z, obtained satisfactory cover of Jahore Bharu and Singapore Island on the 16th.

On 22 July Flt Lt D Warwick and Flg Off G Jowles covered more airfield sites, in RG186/G, at Batu Pahat, Yong Peng and Kluang, in Johore State, Malaya. Four days later Newman and Flt Sgt Pateman, in RG184/X, obtained further airfield coverage of Airmotek, in Sumatra, of Changi on Singapore Island, Tebrau, Batu Pahat and Lumut (Sitiawan), on the west coast. By the end of July 25 sorties had been completed by seven PR 34s of No 2 Detachment. No operations were flown during the first week of August, however, because of bad weather en route to Malaya. Indeed, some of the proposed invasion beaches were never photographed because of high-tides – the photos were only useful if taken at low-tide.

Operation *Zipper* never went ahead, for Japan unconditionally surrendered on 14 August following the dropping of the two atomic bombs on the 6th and 9th on Hiroshima and Nagasaki. The surrender brought added responsibilities for the PR Mosquitoes, which were required to bring back further information on PoW camps and Japanese dispositions in Malaya. Two PR 34s were duly lost, PR XVI NS528 breaking its back as a result of a heavy landing at Alipore on 11 August, and newly-arrived PR 34 RG213/O ditched into the sea at China Bay eight days later whilst attempting to land on one engine. The crews were unhurt, but both aircraft were written off. On the 20th, Flt Lt J R Manners and Wt Off F A Burley, in RG210/J, photographed Penang Island and Taiping, in northern Malaya, during a return trip of 2600 miles on a record 9 hr 5 min flight. The oilfields at Palembang, on Sumatra were also photographed.

After the Japanese surrender on 14 August 1945, the PR Mosquitoes were required to bring back further information on PoW camps and Japanese dispositions in Malaya (*Author's Collection*)

P.W. Camp

77

On 31 August 1945 a PR 34 from Cocos Island flown by Sqn Ldr Cliff G Andrews RNZAF and Wt Off H S Painter photographed Singapore, but developed an engine fault. Rather than risk the long flight back to Cocos, Andrews decided to land at Kallang, on Singapore Island. There, amid great excitement, they were courteously greeted by the Japanese, who arranged for some RAF PoWs in Changi jail to repair the faulty engine. The crew were the first Britons, apart from a British medical officer parachuted into the country to attend to PoWs the previous day, to arrive in Singapore since the surrender.

On 3 September Gen Itazaki, Japanese Southern Area Commander, formerly surrendered to Vice-Adm Lord Louis Mountbatten in Singapore, thus ending the war with Japan. The official history had this say;

'PR in SE Asia was of the greatest importance than in other theatres, owing to the comparatively meagre ground intelligence available, and for the the RAF's purposes alone it provided an indispensable factor in the maintenance of Allied air superiority, a vital factor in the defeat of the Japanese forces.'

After VJ-Day, No 684 used its PR 34s to fly a high-speed courier service throughout the Far East, while small detachments at Mingladon, in Burma, Batavia, in Indonesia, and Labuan, in North Borneo, carried out survey work in the region. Navigator Flt Lt Bill Mc Lintock who, with his

On 31 August 1945 a PR 34 from Cocos Island, flown by Sqn Ldr Cliff G Andrews RNZAF and Wt Off H S Painter, photographed Singapore, but developed an engine fault. Rather than risk the long flight back to Cocos, Andrews decided to land at Kallang, on Singapore Island. There, amid great excitement, they were courteously greeted by the Japanese, who even arranged for some RAF PoWs still in Changi jail (pictured) to repair the faulty engine (*Author's Collection*)

PR 34s of No 684 Sqn at Mingaldon, Burma. The nearest aircraft is RG284/S (*Denis Moore Collection*)

skipper, Flt Lt K 'Sam' Rawcliffe, arrived at Alipore in PR 34 RG253 from the UK on 5 October, recalls;

'Of all the detachments, the most memorable was probably Labaun. We were accommodated in tents and shared the site with a small signals unit. Crews would fly out from Singapore, carrying out a survey en route, and land at Labaun. Some surveys would be carried out from the island and, on the return flight to Singapore, a survey of Sarawak was included. On one memorable trip, Wt Offs McDonald and Radford left Seletar and ran into a typhoon over Borneo, leaving them with insufficient fuel to return to Singapore, and they crash-landed in a rice field in Borneo. It took about ten days to get then back to the squadron.'

By 16 October the China Bay detachment was withdrawn to Indo-China, where a revolt against the French had broken out. On the 19th three of No 684 Sqn's PR 34s and Spitfires of No 273 Sqn flew a demonstration over Dalat, 130 miles to the north-east, where Annamite rebels had taken control. On the 21st, six PR 34s left Alipore for Tan Son Nhut, near Saigon, to provide PR and survey support. Bill McLintock recalls;

'The weather was bad, and at the briefing we were told not to return to Alipore. We climbed through cloud before emerging into clear skies at about 23,000 ft. After about two-and-a-half hours we got a glimpse of the ground, and found that we were very far off course heading south-east, and eventually picked up our position over Siam. I suggested a diversion to Bangkok, but Sam decided to press on, although I pointed out that if we encountered more bad weather our fuel position would be precarious.

'After about five-and-a-half hours we reached Saigon, with the gauges reading almost zero. We were met by Sqn Ldr Newman, and were very surprised to find that we were the first to land. After a period of waiting, a signal arrived stating that three Mossies had diverted to Bangkok. A later signal confirmed that Wg Cdr Lowry, with Gerald Stevens as his navigator, had crashed at Mingladon, on course but with a seized up starboard engine and associated problems. Unfortunately, the Mosquito crewed by Flt Lt Mike Workman and Wt Off Jimmy Fawkner was missing, and was never located. It was later assumed that the plane had crashed into the Bay of Bengal. PR sorties were flown during the subsequent weeks to establish the location and disposition of Annamite rebel forces in the area.'

Early in November 1945 the seven PR 34s on Cocos Island flew to Seletar, Singapore, for survey work in Malaya and the East Indies. Wg Cdr Lowry DFC and Flt Lt George Jones, in PR 34 RG184/X, were lost during the long transit flight, and the newly-promoted Wg Cdr Kos Newman DFC* assumed command of No 684.

At the end of January 1946 No 684 Sqn moved to Don Muang to take up more survey duties. The Seletar detachment stayed until early March, when it too moved to Don Muang. In April Wg Cdr John Merrifield DSO, DFC* assumed command. In May a detachment was sent to Kemajoran, in Java, where a bloody civil war with Indonesian rebels was in progress. No 684 Sqn's main task was to make a four-month topographical survey of Java before the Netherlands East Indies Army finally

took over from the British. In late August No 684 Sqn moved to Seletar where, on 1 September, it disbanded by renumbering as No 81 Sqn. On 1 August 1947 Spitfires were transferred to the unit, which became the sole PR asset in FEAF, and took on the responsibility of PR and aerial survey work for the entire region.

The last RAF Mosquitoes to see RAF service anywhere were the PR 34As of No 81 Sqn at Seletar. In 1946-47 the unit had carried out an aerial survey of the country. A state of emergency in Malaya was declared on 17 June 1948 when a full-scale communist uprising began, and No 81 Sqn's Mosquitoes reverted to their PR role as part of Operation *Firedog*, which began in July 1949.

By the end of 1952 the unit had flown over 4000 sorties and photographed 34,000 square miles. No 81 Sqn flew no less than 6619 sorties during its eight years of operations in Malaya, with the honour of flying the RAF's very last Mosquito mission, on 15 December 1955, going to RG314, and Flg Offs A J 'Collie' Knox and A B 'Tommy' Thompson – the crew successfully completed a *Firedog* reconnaissance sortie against two terrorist camps in Malaya .

No 684 Sqn groundcrew toiling on a Merlin engine in the hot sun (*Denis Moore Collection*)

RAF AND COMMONWEALTH PR MOSQUITO UNITS

No 1 Photo Reconnaissance Unit (8/7/40 to 26/6/43)
Command Assignments: No 16 Group Coastal Command, Bomber Command, 26/6/43
Aircraft: PR I, PR II, PR IV, PR IX, PR XVI and PR 32
History: No 1 PRU was renamed as such from the PDU (Photographic Development Unit) 8/7/42. First Mosquito (PR I) operation 17/9/42, disbanded 19/10/42 and PRU reformed as five PR squadrons, Nos 540 & 544 Sqns being equipped with Mosquitoes. Re-numbered No 106(PR) Wing 26/6/43. Re-numbered again 15/5/44 as No 106(PR) Group (15/5/44-7/5/45)

No 4 Sqn
Motto: *'In futurum videre'* ('To see into the future')
Command Assignments: No 35(R) Wing, No 84 Group, 2nd TAF
Aircraft: (B Flight) PR XVI (12/43-11/5/44)
History: August 1943 received Spitfire XIs and Mosquito XVIs for high-level PR duties. Early 1944 gave up its Mustangs, which it used on

PR 34 VL619, which served in No 13 Sqn at Fayid, Egypt and was SoC in September 1951 (*via Philip Jarrett*)

'Rhubarbs' across the Channel, and went over to PR duties in 2nd TAF using just Spitfires and PR XVIs (B Flight). First Mosquito PR sortie flown 20/3/44. Among the tasks alloted was the need to map all V1 sites in northern France. Last Mosquito sortie flown 20/5/44, further conversion to Spitfires having already begun, 11 May.

No 60 Sqn, SAAF

Motto: '*Per ardua ad aethera tendo*' ('I strive through difficulties to the sky')

Command Assignments: North African Tactical Air Force (No 285 Wing/No 336 Wing), Mediterranean Allied PR Wing, Italy

Aircraft: PR IV (2/43-11/43), PR IX, PR VI and PR XVI (8/43-7/45)

History: Equipped with Baltimores and Marylands in 1942 for PR operations in support of the British 8th Army in the Western Desert. Two PR IV Mosquitoes arrived in February 1943, reputedly on the insistence of Gen Montgomery, to photograph the Mareth Line between Tunisia and Libya. Fitted with American K-17 cameras, ideal for mapping photographs, these being first used operationally on 15 February. Col Owen Glynn Davies was instrumental in getting his squadron equipped with Mosquitoes. In July 1943 a detachment operated from Lentini, south of Catania, Sicily. By November ten PR IXs, and a Mk VI for training, were on the strength of B Flight (LR480 is displayed at the South African National Museum of Military History at Saxonwold). In February 1944 the first of 14 PR XVIs (and two F IIs) arrived. PR flights were made, 1944-45, as far afield as Austria, the Balkans and southern Germany – Me 262 jets accounted for some of the squadron's aircraft lost. Towards the end of the war the unit carried out mapping survey work over Austria, the Alps, Italy and France. Postwar, further survey work was carried out in Greece until 15 July 1945, when ten surviving Mosquitoes were flown to Zwarkop, in South Africa.

No 86 Sqn, RAAF

Command Assignments: RAAF

Aircraft: FB 40 (modified) and PR XVI

Stations: Coomalee Creek, Northern Territory, and Broome, Western Australia

History: Reformed from No 1 PRU RAAF on 10/9/45, equipped with modified FB 40s. No 1 PRU had originally been based in the Northern

PR 34 RG177 of No 81 Sqn beating up Seletar in May 1953. Although this shot is not strictly applicable to this volume, it is too good a PR photo to leave out (*Aeroplane*)

Flg Offs A J 'Collectionie' Knox and A B 'Tommy' Thompson of No 81 Sqn at Seletar were chosen by their CO, Wg Cdr S McCreith AFC, to complete the final operational flight of a Mosquito in the RAF in PR 34A RG314 on 15 December 1955 – a *Firedog* sortie over Malaya (*via Gerry Scutts*)

Territtory of Australia to cover the Dutch East Indies, including East Java, Borneo East, the Celebes, the Halmaheras, Timor, Kai Islands and later the Philippines – especially Davao Gulf and Leyte Gulf. FB 40s were modified to carry cameras, with the first PR 40 sortie flown from Coomalee Creek (54 miles south of Darwin) on 1/6/44. By 1945, Broome (1500 miles west of Coomalee Creek) was being used, enabling the PR 40s and seven British-built PR XVIs (from a batch of 23 – A52-600/-622), to reach targets in East Java, 2300 miles distant, on flights lasting up to nine hours' duration.

No 87 Sqn, RAAF
Command Assignments: No 87 Wing, RAAF
Aircraft: PR 40/FB 40 (modfied) and PR XVI
Stations: Coomalee Creek, Northern Territory, and Parkes, New South Wales
History: Operated six PR 40s (delivered May-October 1944) and 20 FB 40s (delivered 1944-45) on PR in the NW area of the Pacific to photograph Japanese-held territories, including Borneo. The first 12 of 16 PR XVIs received from Britain in March 1945 when No 87 Sqn flew a number of sorties to find, and successfully photograph, the Japanese heavy cruiser *Isuzu* and her three escorts en route to Koepang, Timor Island. PR XVIs used almost exclusively for the rest of the war, although Mk 40s were still used on sorties to Java and East Borneo. Two PR XVIs and one Mk 40, under the command of Sqn Ldr K J 'Red' Gray DFC, detached to RAF Station Brown, Cocos Islands, from June 1945 to photograph Singapore, but bad weather restricted the unit to just one flight, to Christmas Island. Postwar used PR 41 (28 built A52-300/-327, delivered 29/5/47-22/7/48) on a large-scale aerial survey of Australia (A52-319 is displayed at the Australian War Memorial, Canberra). Disbanded on 24 July 1946.

No 140 Sqn

Motto: 'Foresight'

Command Assignments: No 34 (PR) Wing, HQ 2nd TAF (11/43-5/45)

Aircraft: PR IX (11/43-7/44) and PR XVI (12/43-8/45)

History: June 1943 became part of No 34 Wing, 2nd TAF, and produced detailed photography of coastal installations and targets, as well as general mapping. In November 1943 a number of PR IXs introduced for long-range PR, followed by PR XVIs equipped with *Gee* and *Rebecca*. Using this equipment, unit was able to carry out blind night photography. First night sortie flown on 4 May 1944. After the D-Day invasion moved to the continent, first to Amiens, France, and in September to Belgium. Early in 1945 experimented with night photography controlled by a mobile radar post, but the range was limited and needed further development to realise its full potential. In April the squadron switched to visual reconnaissance over the German and Danish coasts as these areas were being liberated. Returned to England in July 1945. Disbanded at Fersfield on 10 November 1945.

No 400 Sqn, RCAF

Motto: '*Percussi vigiles*'

Command Assignments: No 39(R) Wing, No 83 Group, 2nd TAF

Aircraft: (A Flight) PR XVI (12/43-12/5/44)

History: December 1943 A flight began conversion onto Spitfire XIs and B Flight began re-equipment with Mosquito PR XIs purely for reconnaissance duties. B Flight's first Mosquito sortie flown on 26/3/44, the last (43rd) on 2/5/44. Replaced by Spitfires in mid-May 1944.

No 540 Sqn

Motto: '*Sine qua non*' ('Indispensable')

Command Assignments: No 1 PRU (19/10/42), No 106(PR) Wing (26/6/43-15/5/44), No 106(PR) Group (15/5/44-7/5/45)

Aircraft: PR IV (10/42-5/43), PR XI (6/43-5/44) and PR XVI (6/44-9/46)

'B' Flight of No 680 Sqn, pictured at Matariya, Egypt, in November 1944. Seated, are, 'Kev' Kevan (3rd from right), Wg Cdr J C Paish, CO, (12th from right), Plt Off Ron Watson (7th from right), and Flg Off Charles 'Bud' Tingwell (6th from left), the famous postwar Australian TV and film star (*'Kev' Kevan Collection*)

PR 34 RG190 and Spitfire PR XIX of the PR Flight at Benson in 1948
(*D J Mannion via Jerry Scutts*)

History: 19 October 1942 two flights of the PRU (H and L Flights) at Leuchars were merged to form No 540 Sqn. Principally tasked to cover the passage of German capital shipping, operating far and wide throughout Northern and Western Europe and the Mediterranean on this task. 1943, battle-damage assessment and target reconnaissance at such places as Peenemünde became added tasks. Beginning in 1944, went over totally to reconnaissance of the German rail transportation system in preparation for D-Day. By the end of the year detachments had been established at Gibraltar, Agadir, Lossiemouth, Yagodnik, Dyce and Leuchars for reconnaissance of enemy shipping, and in USSR. Moved to Coulommiers, France, March 1945, for complete PR of the country. Finished this assignment November 1945, then returned to Benson, disbanding there 30 September 1946.

No 544 Sqn

Motto: '*Quaero*' ('I Seek')
Command Assignments: No 1 PRU (19/10/42), No 106(PR) Wing (26/6/43-15/5/44), No 106(PR) Group (15/5/44-7/5/45)
Aircraft: PR IV (4/43-9/43) and PR IX (10/43-10/45)
History: Formed at Benson 19/10/42 and equipped with Ansons, Wellington IV and Spitfire PR IV aircraft for PR and night photography roles. In April 1943 PR IVs replaced the Wellingtons, and before the year was out PR IXs completed re-equipment. All were used on day and night photographic missions over Germany, Western Europe, southern France and Austria, using an advance base at San Severo, in Italy. Early in 1944 Mosquitoes ranged over Norway and, in July 1944, were flying regularly to Moscow for sorties over eastern Germany and Poland. In addition, the Black Sea ports and the Balkans were also covered. In 1945 some of the Mosquitoes had their cameras removed and were used to fly diplomatic mail sorties over liberated Europe. After VE-Day, squadron allocated to 'Tiger Force' for the invasion of Japan, but after VJ-Day was switched to aerial survey work over Holland and Belgium. Disbanded at Benson on 13 October 1945.

No 618 Sqn

Command Assignments: *Highball* development
Aircraft: PR XVI (5) (7/44-3/45)
History: Formed 1 April 1943, one month before No 617 Sqn's attack on the German dams (16/17 May) for the sole purpose of using 950-lb, 35-in diameter, *Highball* weapons against the *Tirpitz* and other 'major naval units and other shipping at sea'. Strike was called off and unit re-tasked for re-assignment to Pacific Theatre, summer 1944, for attacks

from aircraft carriers against Japanese shipping. Five crews and three PR XVIs provided by Nos 540 and 544 Sqns to find the enemy ships, despatched with 24 B IVs to Australia on 31 October 1944 in the carriers *Fencer* and *Striker*, arriving in Melbourne on 23 December. Moved to Narromine, New South Wales, February 1945 to begin operations, but a shortage of suitable shipping targets saw the squadron remain in Australia until 14 July 1945, when it disbanded at Narromine.

No 680 Sqn

Command Assignments: Middle-East/Mediterranean

Aircraft: PR IX (2/44-3/45) and PR XVI (2/44-9/46)

History: On 1/2/43 No 2 PRU was re-numbered No 680 Sqn and made part of the new Mediterranean Air Command, formed 23/2/43. Received PR IX LR444 16 February 1944 (MIA 28/2/45 over Crete, Plt Off Ted Ousley killed when parachute candled, Wt Off Cyril Butterworth survived), followed next day by the first of nine PR XVIs (all arrived by April). Beginning 7 May 1944, carried out PR in the eastern Mediterranean and Greece (B Flight, Tocra) and Balkans (A Flight, San Severo) using PR IXs and PR XVIs. To San Severo in August 1944, from where Mosquitoes ranged over the Balkans and Hungary, before finishing the war mapping Italy. Moved to Egypt in February 1945 to work solely as a survey unit, and then to Palestine to survey that country, before finally disbanding at Ein Shemer on 13 September 1946 by renumbering as No 13 Sqn.

No 681 Sqn

Command Assignments: India-Burma

Aircraft: PR IX (8/43-12/43)

History: Formed at Dum Dum 2/1/43. Used Hurricanes, Spitfire IVs and Mitchells, before adding a few Mosquitoes as a temporary measure in August 1943. Operated just Spitfire IVs and XIs in 1944. Disbanded in India on 1 August 1946 by renumbering as No 34 Sqn.

No 682 Sqn

Command Assignments: North Africa

Aircraft: PR II and PR VI (4/43-8/43)

History: Formed at Maison Blanche on 1/2/43 by renumbering No 4 PRU. Equipped with Spitfires, and in 4/43 some PR Mosquitoes for longer range operations were acquired – the first Mosquito operation, over the French Alps, was flown on 20/5. Almost all PR sorties in July were flown over Italian airfields, and by August all Mosquitoes were withdrawn.

No 683 Sqn

Motto: '*Nihil nos latet*' ('Nothing Escapes Us')

Command Assignments: Middle East

Aircraft: F II and FB VI (5/43-6/43)

History: Formed at Luqa 8/2/43 from B Flight of No 69 Sqn. Initially equipped with Spitfire PR IVs and later PR XIs, before adding Mosquito F IIs and FB Vis in 5/43 for a month of operations over Italy and Sicily, starting on the 13th.

No 684 Sqn
Motto: 'Invisus videns'
Command Assignments: India-Burma
Aircraft: F II (11/43-12/43), FB VI (11/43-8/44), PR IX (10/43-7/44), PR XVI (2/44-2/46) and PR 34 (7/45-9/46)
History: Formed Dum Dum 29/9/43 from the twin-engined flights of No 681 Sqn, and equipped from the outset with F IIs, FB VIs and PR IXs, as well as Mitchell III aircraft. Flew long-range PR sorties during the Burma campaign, regularly going to the Andaman islands, Rangoon and the Burma-Thailand railway. Performed survey flying using PR IXs and PR XVIs from Calcutta, before moving to Alipore for the remainder of the war. Detachments sent to the Cocos Islands, Ceylon and Burma until VJ-Day. Then continued to operate PR 34s, providing a high-speed courier service to the far flung units in the Far East, before moving to Bangkok in 1/46 to undertake survey duties. Disbanded 1/9/46 by re-numbering as No 81 Sqn.

MISCELLANEOUS UNITS

No 1 PRU
No 8 PR OTU
Special Flying Unit
No 1 PRU RAAF
Photographic Development Unit

APPENDICES

WARTIME MOSQUITO RECONNAISSANCE SQUADRONS/UNITS

Squadron	Theatre	Period	Type(s)
No 1 PRU	GB	17/9/41-10/42	PR I/II/IV
No 1 PRU RAAF	Australia	6/44-10/9/45	FB 40(mod)
No 4 (B Flt)	2nd TAF	12/43-5/44	PR XVI
No 60 SAAF	Italy	8/43-7/45	PR IX, FB VI, PR XVI
No 86 RAAF	Australia	10/9/45-1946	FB 40(mod), PR XVI
No 87 RAAF	Australia	5/44-7/46	FB 40(mod), PR XVI
No 140	2nd TAF	11/43-11/45	PR IX/XVI
No 400 RCAF (A Flt)	2nd TAF	12/43-12/5/44	PR XVI
No 521	GB	8/42-31/3/43	PR IV
No 543	GB	6/43-10/43	PR IV (training)
No 544	GB	4/43-10/45	PR IV/IX/XVI/32/34
No 540	GB	10/42-9/46	PR IV/IX/XVI
No 618	Australia	7/44 -3/45	PR XVI (5)
No 680	Middle East/Mediterranean	16/2/44-31/8/46	PR IX/XVI
No 681	India	8/43-11/43	PR II/IV
No 682	North Africa	5/43-7/43	PR IX
No 683	Malta	5/43-6/43	PR IV
No 684	Far East	29/9/43-31/8/46	PR II/VI/IX/XVI/34
653rd BS USAAF* (WR)	GB	7/44-5/45	PR XVI
654th BS USAAF* (PR)	GB	7/44-5/45	PR XVI

Notes

*25th BG also received 16 F 8 versions that were never unused
WR – Weather Reconnaissance
PR – Photo Reconnaissance

MISCELLANEOUS MOSQUITO UNITS

Pathfinder Navigation Training Unit (PFFNTU)
Photographic Development Unit
No 8 PR OTU
Special Flying Unit

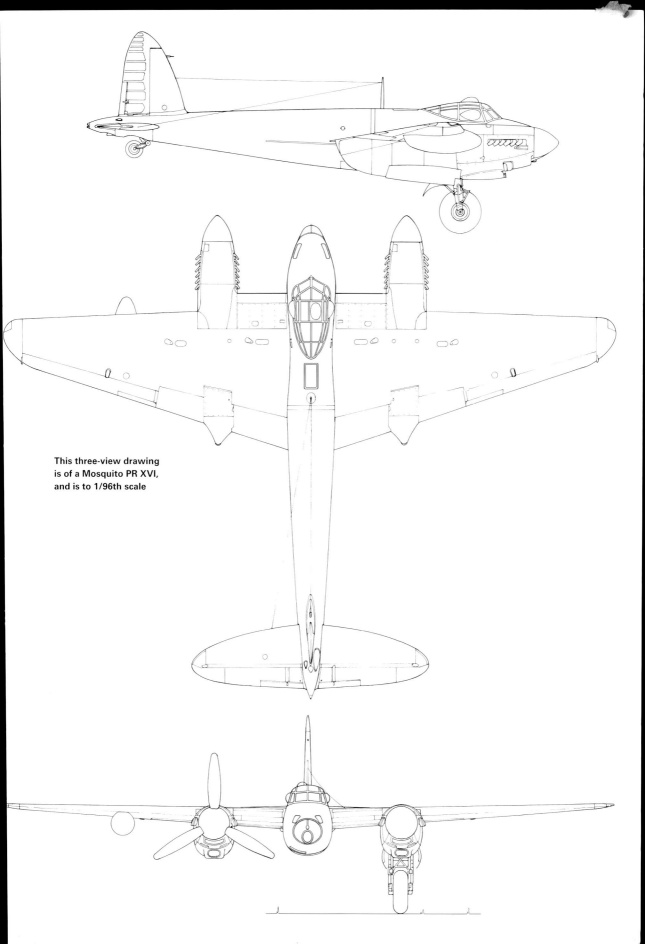

This three-view drawing
is of a Mosquito PR XVI,
and is to 1/96th scale

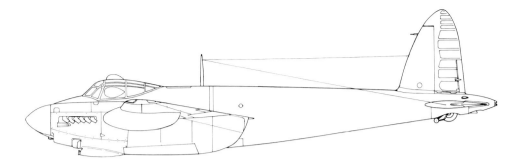

Mosquito PR XVI

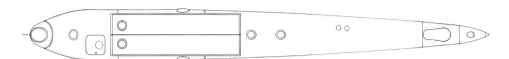

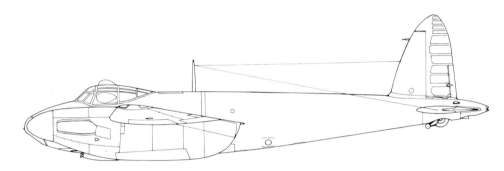

Mosquito PR I

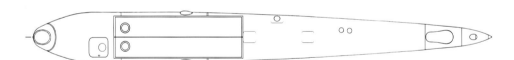

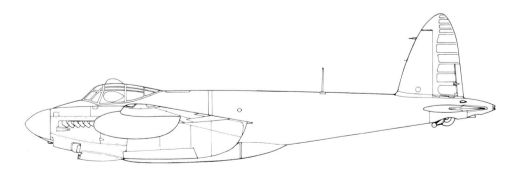

Mosquito PR 34

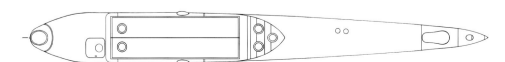

1
PR I W4051 of No 1 PRU, RAF Benson, August 1943

PR I prototype W4051 flew for the first time on 10 June 1941. It reached the Aeroplane & Armaments Experimental Establishment (A&AEE) at Boscombe Down on 28 June, and on 13 July was handed over to No 1 PRU, where it became the first Mosquito to be taken on charge by the RAF. The Mosquito then went to Hatfield for adjustments, returning on 10 August. W4051 was one of four transferred to operate from Wick, in Scotland, where it flew sorties over Norway. On 20 February 1942 W4051 was flown to the Franco-Spanish border, and over marshalling yards and airfields at Toulouse, in southern France. It also photographed the French coast prior to the commando raid on St Nazaire. On 20 September 1942 it joined No 521 Sqn at Bircham Newton, Norfolk, returning to Benson, and No 540 Sqn, ten days later. On 31 August 1943 the Mosquito was passed onto No 8 OTU at Dyce to serve as an aircrew trainer. W4051 crashed on 19 July 1944 and was returned to Hatfield for repairs, but was instead SoC on 22 June 1945.

2
PR I W4055/LY-N *Benedictine* of No 1 PRU, flown by Sqn Ldr Rupert Clerk and Sgt Sowerbutts, RAF Benson, 17 September 1941

PR I W4055 joined No 1 PRU at Benson on 8 August 1941, was coded LY-N, and later named *Benedictine*. On 17 September, Sqn Ldr Rupert Clerke and Sgt Sowerbutts made the first successful PR I sortie when they set out in W4055 for a daylight PR of Brest, La Pallice and Bordeaux. W4055 was one of four aircraft transferred to Scotland for sorties over Norway, and failed to return on 4 December 1941 with Sqn Ldr Alastair L 'Ice' Taylor DFC, and his navigator, Sgt Sidney E Horsfall, aboard, while covering Trondheim and Bergen.

3
PR I W4059/LY-T of No 1 PRU, flown by Flg Off Victor Ricketts and Sgt Boris Lukhmanoff, RAF Benson, 24 April 1942

W4059 was coded LY-T in No 1 PRU (where it flew 59 PR sorties before joining No 540 Sqn in October 1942). It was one of four PR Is modified with increased fuel tankage for long-range operations, and was transferred to operate from Wick for sorties over Norway. On 2 March 1942, W4059 photographed the *Gneisenau* and, on 24 April, Flg Off Victor Ricketts and Sgt Boris Lukhmanoff used W4059 to take photos of the Lancaster daylight raid on the MAN works at Augsburg. On 26 January 1943, Flt Lts Bill White RCAF and Ron Prescott used W4059 to search in vain for the *Scharnhorst* from Sogne Fjord down to Stavanger, flying at ,000 ft. The aircraft subsequently joined

No 8 OTU, before being SoC on 20 September 1944.

4
PR IV DZ411/G-AGFV used by BOAC from December 1942 to 5 January 1945

DZ411 was one of two PR IVs (conversions of existing B IV Series II bombers) which joined No 540 Sqn in December 1942. On 15 December, registered G-AGFV, it became the first Mosquito to be used by BOAC. On 23 April 1943 it landed at Barkaby, Sweden, with hydraulic problems caused by enemy action, and was returned to service on 10 December 1943. On 14 May 1944 its wheel brakes burst as a result of pulling up sharply, indirectly caused by the excessive heating of the port engine radiator. On 4 July 1944, whilst at Stockholm, the airspeed indicator went u/s and the aircraft swung off the runway, where its undercarriage collapsed. DZ411 returned to the RAF on 6 January 1945 and was eventually SoC on 10 October 1946.

5
PR IV DZ473 of No 540 Sqn, flown by Flt Lts Bill White, RCAF, and Ron Prescott, RAF Benson, 22 April 1943

DZ473 (a B IV Series II converted into a PR IV) was used by Flt Lts Bill White RCAF and Ron Prescott on their 22nd sortie, flown on 22 April 1943, to photograph the railyards at Stettin. They left their cameras running as they flew down the north coast of Germany, and when the film was developed, it was found to contain pictures of Peenemünde. On 12 June a sortie in DZ473 by Flt Lt Reggie A Lenton resulted in the first definite evidence that previously unidentified objects seen at the base were in fact V2 rockets. DZ473 ended its days with No 8 OTU, where it was lost on 22 January 1944 when it spun in and crashed near Middleton St George airfield, killing both crew.

6
PR IV DK310/E-42, formerly of No 1 PRU, flown by Flt Lt Gerry R Wooll, RCAF, and Sgt John Fielden, RAF Benson, 24 August 1942

PR IV DK310 was used on 24 August 1942 by Flt Lt Gerry R Wooll, RCAF, and Sgt John Fielden of No 1 PRU to cover Italy, and obtain photos of Venice, which were needed to confirm a report that Italian warships were putting to sea. DK310 proceeded uneventfully to Venice, but when the starboard engine quit, Wooll was forced to head for Switzerland, where he force-landed at Berne-Belp airfield. The crew were interned for four months before being repatriated in an exchange deal which allowed two interned Bf 109 pilots to leave for Germany. DK310 was retained by the Swiss air force, who coded it E-42 and evaluated it at Lucerne-Emmen – it was officially sold to the Swiss by the British government on 3 July 1944.

Given to Swissair (and coded HB-IMO) for the training of civil pilots on night mail runs that, in event, did not materialise, the aircraft was returned to the air force. Recoded B-4, it was sporadically used until 21 August 1946, when it was stored for a number of years before being scrapped.

7

PR IX LR416 of No 540 Sqn, flown by squadron commander, Wg Cdr Lord Malcolm-Hamilton OBE, 11 August 1943

PR IX LR416 was delivered to No 540 Sqn on 4 July 1943, and it set out on its first operation on 10 August, for northern Italy, although the mission was abandoned when a problem with the drop tanks developed. Next day, Wg Cdr Lord Malcolm Douglas-Hamilton OBE, the unit's CO, used LR416 to photograph Friedrickshafen, before he landed at La Marsa, in Italy. He made the return flight on 15 August. The aircraft flew ten sorties in 1943, and on 25 March 1944 obtained photos of the 'Siegfried Line'. On 13 April 1944 it took off on its eighth sortie of the year, leaving Benson for Munich at 0950. A problem developed and the crew were forced to return, and it was destroyed in a crash two miles from Kingston Bagpuize aerodrome, in Oxfordshire, when a wing came off while diving out of cloud. The primary cause was the detachment of the escape hatch in the high-speed dive.

8

PR XI LR417 of 544 Sqn, flown by squadron commander, Sqn Ldr J R H Merrifield DFC and Flg Off W N Whalley, RAF Benson, 4 October 1943

PR IX LR417 flew its first operation in No 544 Sqn on 4 October 1943 when Sqn Ldr J R H Merifield DFC and Flg Off W N Whalley flew to Berlin. On 6 October LR417 was intercepted over Utrecht, but managed to out-distance its pursuers. On 12 October 1943 Sqn Ldr Merrifield flew LR417 to Trier, Regensburg, Linz, Vienna, Budapest, back to Vienna, Sarbonon, Bucharest, Foggia and to Catalania, where it ran out of fuel as he taxied in. LR417 flew its 64th, and final, sortie on 29 November 1944.

9

PR IX LR424 of No 540 Sqn, flown by Plt Off R A Hosking, RAF Benson, 28 October 1942

PR IX LR424 arrived at No 27 MU on 22 July 1943 and was allocated to No 540 Sqn on 7 September 1943. Plt Off R A Hosking used LR424 to photograph the V1 flying-bomb launching site at Bois Carrq, ten miles north-east of Abbeville, on 28 October 1942. This was the first V1 site to be analysed on photographs. Sqn Ldr J R H Merrifield DFC tried to photograph Berlin in this aircraft on 25 September 1943 but was forced to abort when the German capital was covered in thick cloud. He noted vapour trails rising from Peenemünde during this same flight. BDA sorties to Berlin were flown in December, and on the 17th, LR424's

photos revealed progress at Peenemünde. On 20 December LR424 photographed Peenemünde again. The aircraft subsequently failed to return from a PR sortie to Friedrichshafen on 10 April 1944.

10

PR IX LR429 of No 540 Sqn, flown by Flt Lt Ken W 'Osk' Watson, RAAF, and Flg Off Ken H Pickup, RAFVR, RAF Benson, 4 September 1944

PR IX LR429 of No 540 Sqn was flown by Flt Lt Ken W 'Osk' Watson RAAF and Flg Off Ken H Pickup RAFVR on 4 September 1944. At 29,000 ft, Pickup was in the nose preparing to film railway lines between Nürnburg and Munich when he spotted just 600 yards away an He 280 jet fighter, approaching from starboard. Watson instantly took evasive action by making tight turns to port, but the enemy aircraft disappeared from view. Almost immediately its place was taken by an Me 262, 500 yards to port. Now back in his seat, kneeling and facing aft, Pickup sighted a second Me 262 about 1000 yards to port. The jets attacked simultaneously, and for 15 minutes LR429 evaded them. At 3000 ft one Me 262 broke off and flew away. Watson dived to zero feet and the other Me 262 followed down to 1500 ft and stayed with them for a while. LR429 hit the tip of a Bavarian pine tree, which shattered the nose perspex, filled the cockpit with pine needles and let in a freezing cold draught. Despite the uncomfortable conditions, the crew pressed on through the Brenner Pass to San Severo, Italy. LR429 touched down at 1305, and the crew got out covered in pine needles looking like two 'blue hedgehogs'! After repairs were effected using marine plywood and ship's canvas, LR429 took off for the return flight to Benson but the left undercarriage failed to retract, leaving Watson with little choice but to crash-land the aircraft. The crew survived unscathed, but LR429 had to be written off.

11

PR IX LR432 of No 544 Sqn, flown by Flt Lt J C Webb and Plt Off C D Smith, RAF Benson, 29 November 1944

PR IX LR432 was delivered to No 540 Sqn on 4 September 1943. On 15 September it was used to fly No 544 Sqn's inaugural PR IX operation, before being transferred to No 544 Sqn on 8 October. On 17 September Sqn Ldr John Merrifield flew it to Poznan. He tried to repeat the flight the next day, but collided with a flock of birds and had to turn back. On 21 October Wg Cdr Lord Malcolm Douglas-Hamilton flew it to Lyons and photographed part of the Pyrenees. LR432 made a 5hr 20min flight to Besancon and Nancy on 29 December. On 21 August 1944, Wg Cdr D W Steventon DSO, DFC (the unit's CO) flew LR432 on a low-level sortie to Ijmuiden RDF station. On 6 October 1944 a fighter chased the Mosquito over Utrecht and Lingen. Flt Lt J C Webb and Plt Off C D Smith flew LR432 on its 43rd, and final, operation, to Hemmingstadt and Heligoland, on 29 November

1944. On 22 January 1945 the veteran aircraft passed to No 8 OTU. It was finally SoC on 11 September 1945.

12

PR IX LR480 *Lovely Lady/Anne!* of No 60 Sqn, SAAF, flown by Col Owen Glynn Davies and Brig Hingeston, Italy, 14 December 1944

LR480 was taken on strength by the RAF at Benson on 10 November 1943, and a month later was prepared for overseas duty and flown to the Middle East. On 8 June 1944 LR480 joined No 60 Sqn SAAF at Foggia, and it flew many sorties over the Balkans and Austria. On 14 December 1944 Col Owen Glynn Davies, a former CO of No 60 Sqn, flew an attempted record-breaking flight in LR480 from Cairo to Pretoria with Brig Hingeston as observer, but the Mosquito was damaged when it ran off the end of the 2000-ft long airstrip at Que Que, in Rhodesia. The undercarriage and propellers were replaced and LR480 was flown to South Africa, where it was later donated to the South African National Museum of Military History at Saxonwold, Johannesburg.

13

PR IX LR455/R of No 684 Sqn, flown by Flt Lt K J 'Kos' Newman and Flt Sgt Ray Smith, India, 6 May 1944

On 10 April 1944, Wt Off J A Johnson and Flt Sgt F Wells in No 684 Sqn carried out post target reconnaissance of the Sittang bridge on the Burma railway in LR445/F, and brought back photos that showed that the two western spans of the bridge had been destroyed in a bombing raid two days earlier. Operating from an advanced landing ground at Ramu, on 6 May 1944, Flt Lt K J 'Kos' Newman and Flt Sgt Ray Smith used LR445 (now coded 'R') to photograph Nancowry Harbour, in Great Nicobar. This 2256-mile round trip was at the extreme range of the PR IX. They returned, just, for the last ten minutes of the flight saw the fuel gauges reading zero. LR445 was SoC on 5 July 1944.

14

F-8 43-34926 (KB315) '*The Spook*' of the 3rd PG(R), Twelfth Air Force, Italy, 1944

Canadian-built F8-DH, (KB315) 43-34926 was one of six converted from the B VII. It was delivered by Maj J F Letchell (later Lt Col, Group CO, 4/11/43-18/1/44) and Capt J C Alexander. In March 1943 No 680 Sqn and the 3rd PG, equipped with F-4 and F-5 aircraft (PR version of the P-38 Lightning), formed the North African PR Wing, under the unified command of Lt Col Elliot Roosevelt. Only 34 F-8s (converted from B XX) ever reached the USAAF, these aircraft proving very unpopular with the Americans in England.

15

PR XVI prototype DZ540 of the A&AEE, Farnborough, late August 1943

B IV Series II DZ540 first flew in the summer of 1943, and was sent to the A&AEE in late August to be converted into the prototype PR XVI, powered by Merlin 72/73 engines. At Farnborough, it was used on performance, handling and pressure cabin tests, before returning to de Havilland at Hatfield in July 1944 for overhaul. DZ540 was SoC on 28 July 1945.

16

PR XVI NS777 of No 140 Sqn, 2nd TAF, flown by Flt Lts Arthur T Kirk and A G 'Tony' Humphryes, Melsbroek, 29 December 1944

PR XVI NS777 of No 140 Sqn, 2nd TAF, at Melsbroek, flown on 29 December 1944 by Flt Lts Arthur T Kirk and A G 'Tony' Humphryes on their first operation together a daylight sortie to the Gröningen area and the German border, diverting to B 80 Völkel when Belgium was fogged in. They finished their tour on 3 March 1945.

17

PR XVI MM397 of No 540 Sqn, flown Flt Lt George Watson and Wt Off John McArthur, RAF Benson, September 1944

No 540 Sqn's Flt Lt (later Sqn Ldr) George Watson and Wt Off John McArthur flew PR XVI MM397 in September 1944 to Yagodnik, in the USSR, to act as a weather and reconnaissance scout for the No 5 Group Lancaster attack on the *Tirpitz*. The crew made an an successful PR on 14 September, and on the day of the actual attack (15 September), considerable damage to the battleship was caused, but smoke and cloud prevented any photos being taken. On the 16th MM397 was holed in five places by flak. Both men returned to the UK, where they were each awarded the DFC. Later, MM397 was inscribed with the *Owl Like Us* motif on the nose.

18

PR XVI NS851/H of No 680 Sqn, Italy, 1944

The rudder striping on this aircraft was applied to try to prevent PR Mosquitoes from being attacked by US fighters after the latter had mistakenly identified them as Luftwaffe Me 210s and 410s.

19

PR XVI NS594/U of the 8th WRS(P)Light/802nd BG(P), RAF Watton, June 1944

By June 1944, Mosquitoes in the 802nd BG(P) were organised into the 8th (R) Sqn (P), Special, and the 8th WRS, Light. An 18-inch high radio-call letter was painted on the tail of each aircraft in white and, on Mosquitoes of the Weather Squadron, this was also framed in a white circle, 30 inches in diameter.

20

PR XVI MM345/Z of the 635rd BS/25th BG(R), 325th Photographic Wing, RAF Watton, August 1944

By August 1944 the 802nd (P) had become the 25th BG(R), 325th Photographic Wing, with the 8th RS becoming the 654th BS, Heavy, Special, and the

8th WRS, Light, becoming the 653rd BS, Light. After attacks by Mustangs in July and early August 1944, the vertical tail of the Mosquitoes was painted red and the white circle on the 653rd BS aircraft painted out, leaving the call letter on a circular background of PRU Blue. MM345 was passed to No 10 MU on 16 June 1945, and then SoC on 25 July.

21

PR XVI NS538/F 'Mickey ship' of the 654th BS/25th BG, 325th Photographic Wing, RAF Watton, September 1944

H2X-nosed PR XVI NS538/F of the 654th BS was one of five 'Mickey ships' operated by the 25th BG. Combat missions flown by the 654th BS were usually signified by a camera and flare bomb symbol painted on the port side of the nose. NS538 crashed on 8 September 1944.

22

PR XVI RF992/R of the 654th BS/25th BG, 325th Photographic Wing, flown by Lt Roger W Gilbert and Lt Raymond G Spoerl, RAF Watton, 20 March 1945

On 20 March 1945 this aircraft, flown by Lt Roger W Gilbert and Lt Raymond G Spoerl, was one of four Mosquitoes, flying at 26,000 ft, positioned ahead and below the bomber formation in order to dispense Chaff along the path of the attackers as they headed for Hamburg. The Mosquitoes were attacked by Me 262s, which shot one down, and sent RF992 spiralling out of control after 30 mm cannon hits blew the left wing tip off and put the aileron (and radio) out of action. However, by keeping a much higher power setting on the left engine than the right, Gilbert brought RF992 home safely to Watton.

23

PR XVI NS568/B of the 654th BS/25th BG, 325th Photographic Wing, flown by Lt Otto E Kaellner and Lt Edwin R Cerrutti, RAF Watton, 6/7 November 1944

PR XVI NS568/B was lost, along with 1Lt Otto E Kaellner and Lt Edwin R Cerrutti, on 6/7 November 1944 when they crashed near to home upon returning from a night mission to Cologne.

24

PR XVI NS502 of No 544 Sqn, RAF Benson, 23 May 1944

PR XVI NS502 was delivered to No 544 Sqn on 23 May 1944 and operated over Europe until it crashlanded on 21 February 1945. It then passed to Martin Hearn for repair and was eventually transferred to the Royal Navy at RNAS Fleetlands on 7 November 1947.

25

PR XVI NS519/P of the 653rd BS/25th BG, 325th Photographic Wing, RAF Watton, 1944

PR XVI NS519/P, of the 653rd BS, was used by Lt Earl L Muchway and Lt Lionel Proulux as one of two US Mosquito crews that accompanied the B-17s on the disastrous Frantic Joe shuttle mission to the USSR, Italy and then back to England between 21 June and 5 July 1944. After take-off from San Severo, in Italy, on 5 July, NS519 was forced to abort the flight back at 25,000 ft when the port propeller ran away. The aircraft was repaired by an RAF unit back in Italy, and the crew returned to Watton alone a few days later.

26

PR XVI MM389/P of the 654th BS/25th BG, 325th Photographic Wing, RAF Watton, winter 1944-45

During the winter of 1944-45, 654th BS aircraft that were used on special Joker night reconnaissance missions had their undersides painted gloss reflective black in a US paint known as 'Jet', which had been developed for the P-61 Black Widow. After the loss of three aircraft and crews in three successive night missions, the flights were switched to daylight hours.

27

PR XVI TA614/R of the 492nd BG 'Carpetbaggers', Harrington, March 1945

PR XVI TA614/R was delivered to the USAAF in March 1945 and assigned to the 492nd BG 'Carpetbaggers' at Harrington, which had assumed control of 25th BG Mosquito operations. It is painted overall gloss reflective 'Jet' black for Red Stocking operations to record UHF transmissions from OSS agents on the continent using the 'Joan-Eleanor' device.

28

PR XVI A52-600 of No 87(PR) Sqn, RAAF, flown by Plt Off Allan Davies and Flg Off John Reynolds, Coomalee Creek airstrip, Northern Territory, 23 March 1945

A52-600 was one of 23 PR XVIs built at Hatfield for the RAAF. It was shipped to Australia, arriving in December 1944, and was reassembled and flight tested at No 2 Aircraft Depot, Richmond, NSW. Flown to Coomalee Creek airstrip, NT, it became one of 16 PR XVIs eventually allotted to No 87 (PR) Sqn. Its first operational flight was to Timor on 23 March 1945, and its last, on 11 August, to Kuching prison camp whilst on detachment to Labaun Island, Borneo. Its service record included 21 missions over enemy targets on the Indonesian Archipeligo (as far as Surabaya) and the Borneo invasion. A further 19 missions were completed postwar during the aerial mapping of Australia. A52-600 was withdrawn from flying in 1947 and became a static instructional unit at the Air and Ground Radio School in Ballarat. It was acquired by Mildura Warbirds Aviation Museum in 1966 and kept under cover for 17 years, until returned to the RAAF in 1987. Restoration was then begun to refurbish the aircraft so as to allow it be put on static display, air force receiving much help from the Mosquito Aircraft Association of Australia, and in particular, Allan Davies and John Reynolds, both of whom had flown A52-600 in 1945.

29

PR XVI MM387/U of No 684 Sqn, India, 1945

Airframe and adhesive problems in late 1944 led to a recommendation by J G Fisher of ICI that all Mosquitoes in South-East Asia should be finished overall dull aluminium as a means of reducing the heat absorption of the aircraft's upper surfaces. Supported by de Havilland, the proposal was accepted by the Air Ministry and an Instruction, dated 15 February 1945, ordered that all FB VIs should be given two coats of Aluminium finish overall, while the PR XVIs should be similarly finished on upper surfaces only, remaining PRU blue beneath. However, a number of PR Mosquitoes, still under inspection and repair at No 1 CMU, in Kanchrapara, were repainted overall aluminium like the FB VIs. This aircraft has 28-in, dull blue, wing and tail bands as required for non-camouflaged aircraft as per a Command Instruction issued on 10 March 1945.

30

PR 34 RG184/X of No 2 Detachment, No 684 Sqn, flown by Sqn Ldr K J 'Kos' Newman and Flt Sgt Stan Pateman, Cocos Islands, 26 July 1945

RG184/X was one of seven No 684 Sqn PR 34s of No 2 Detachment based in the Cocos Islands in July 1945. On 26 July Sqn Ldr K J 'Kos' Newman and Flt Sgt Stan Pateman, in RG184/X, obtained airfield coverage of Airmotek. in Sumatra, Changi and Tebrau, on Singapore Island, Batu Pahat and Lumut (Sitiawan), on the west coast of Malaya. Early in November the seven PR 34s flew to Seletar, Singapore, in order to carry out survey work in Malaya and the East Indies. Wg Cdr W E M Lowry DFC and Flt Lt George Jones were subsequently lost in RG184/X during the long transit flight, leaving the newly-promoted Wg Cdr Kos Newman DFC* to assume command of No 684 Sqn.

31

FB 40 A52-101 *SU-Z/SUZIE* of No 87 (Photo Survey) Sqn, RAAF, 1946

FB 40s were modified to carry two F24 split-vertical cameras, an F52 vertical camera mounted in the bomb bay, two additional fuel tanks of 126 gallons' capacity in the bomb-bay and two drop tanks. They were used on a handful of sorties to Java and East Borneo just prior to the Japanese surrender.

32

PR 40 A52-6 of No 87(PR) Sqn, RAAF, Coomalee Creek, Northern Territory, May-October 1944

PR 40 A52-6 was one of six Bankstown-built FB 40s converted to PR 40 specification between May and October 1944 for the RAAF, and was subsequently operated by No 87(PR) Sqn at Coomalee Creek.

33

PR 41 A52-306 of No 87(Photo Survey) Sqn, RAAF, Fairbairn, Canberra, 1950

PR 41 A52-306 was one of 28 aircraft delivered between 29 May 1947 and 22 July 1948 to No 87 (Photo Survey) Sqn, based at RAAF Fairbairn, Canberra. In 1950, it was extensively used during a large-scale aerial survey of Australia carried out by the air force.

FIGURE PLATES

1

Wt Off 'Kev' Kevan of No 680 Sqn at Matariya in 1944. No specially dedicated flying kit was issued to aircrew flying in the Mediterranean and North Africa, PR Mosquito pilots and navigators wearing a mix of European theatre flying kit, locally bought or locally-modified clothing and normal tropical ground uniform, depending on conditions. For example, Kevan is depicted wearing a pair of normal khaki drill trousers and a khaki drill shirt. However, when flying ops he always wore standard RAF Battledress, as shown in figures' two and three. In 1945 the RAF began issuing the Breadon Suit (Flying Overalls, Lightweight, Tropical) to crews, but these were exclusively for use in the Far East. Kevan also wears his normal service pattern shoes, although when on ops he reverted to 1943 Pattern flying/escape boots.

2

Sgt Frank Baylis of No 544 Sqn at RAF Benson in 1944. The RAF Battledress was originally known as the 'Suit, Blue Grey, Aircrew (Blouse and Trousers)', and was originally issued in 1941 to aircrew only specifically for wear in the air. By 1944, the Battledress was in common use by ground personnel as well, and was often worn during ground duties by aircrew. Baylis wears a normal dress shirt, with a black RAF tie, and 1943 Pattern flying/escape boots. These consisted of a basic shoe, with a removable sheepskin-lined suede upper. This had an offset zip, deliberately placed away from the shoe's laces. The young navigator wears the usual bulky RAF Mae West life preserver, with tapes running below the crotch to prevent it riding up. Over this he wears a standard bomber-pattern parachute harness. Finally, Baylis is carrying a standard issue navigator's hold-all, which would have been stuffed full of maps and code books.

3

Flt Lt 'Danny' Daniels of No 544 Sqn at RAF Benson in 1944. He is seen wearing the same basic kit as his navigator, with the standard Battledress 'blouse' jacket, war service dress trousers, 1943 Pattern escape boots and a Mae West. He has discarded his parachute harness, however. The war service dress (Battledress) trousers featured a simple front pocket, closed with a single button. Daniels wears a normal shirt under his Battledress blouse, but has removed its collar and, accordingly, wears no tie. The pilot has tucked a map into his right flying boot, where it could still easily be reached when strapped into his seat.

4

Lt John M Carter, of the 654th BS/25th BG at RAF Watton in 1944, is wearing an A-4 coverall over a regulation Olive Drab uniform shirt and trousers. The shirt has a lieutenant's rank bars on the collar, and Carter is wearing a khaki tie. His goatskin flying gloves are A-10s, lined with camel hair. Carter has yet to finish 'kitting up' for the impending flight.

5

Lt John L Swingen, of the 652nd BS/25th BG at RAF Watton in 194,4 is not dressed for the cockpit of a Mosquito. Instead, he is wearing USAAF officers' Olive Drab slacks and shirt, with a khaki tie, over which he has donned a a light 'wind cheater' jacket. His overseas cap is piped around the turn-up in orange, which was the official AAF colour. Finally, Swingen wears a smartly-shined pair of GI shoes

6

Lt Robert P 'Paddy' Walker, of the 654th BS/25th BG at RAF Watton in 1944, is depicted wearing a regulation woollen shirt and trousers, with heavyweight russet brown GI service shoes. Over his shirt he is wearing a characteristic goatskin A-2 flying jacket, with knitted cuffs and waistband. His Mae West is of a B-3 or B-4 pattern, and he has strapped on a standard USAAF-issue seat parachute on a B-5 harness. As a Mosquito pilot, Walker wears an RAF C-type leather flying helmet with a dedicated H-type mask. The latter was designed specifically for aircrew flying high altitude reconnaissance aircraft. Finally, Walker's goggles are USAF pattern B-7s.

BIBLIOGRAPHY

Birtles, P. *Mosquito - The Illustrated History*. Sutton, 1998

Bishop, E. *Mosquito - The Wooden Wonder*. Airlife, 1995

Bowman, M. W. *The Men Who Flew The Mosquito*. PSL, 1995

Howe, S. *The de Havilland Mosquito*. Aston, 1992

Kirk DFC, A. T. *Names, Ranks & The Blue Mosquitos*. self, 1994

Leaf, E. *Above All Unseen*. PSL, 1997

McKee, A. *The Mosquito Log*. Souvenir Press, 1988

Mosquito Aircrew Assoc. *The Mossie* Vol 10. April 1995

Mosquito Aircrew Assoc. *The Mossie* Vol 11. August 1997

Mosquito Aircrew Assoc. *The Mossie* Vol 12. January 1996

Mosquito Aircrew Assoc. *The Mossie* Vol 16. April 1997

Sharp, C. M. & Bowyer, M. J. F. *Mosquito*. Crecy Books, 1995

Smith, D. J. *DH Mosquito* Crash Log. Midland Counties, 1980

Thomas, G. *Eye of The Phoenix*. Aircraft Modelworld